A CHILD OF BLISS

To my parents
Mervyn Peake and Maeve Gilmore,
writers and artists.

GROWING UP WITH
MERVYN PEAKE

A CHILD OF BLISS

Sebastian Peake

Lennard Publishing

1989

LENNARD PUBLISHING
a Division of Lennard Books Limited
Musterlin House,
Jordan Hill Road,
Oxford, OX2 8DP.

British Library Cataloguing in Publication Data
is available for this title.

ISBN 1 85291 057 7

First published 1989
© Sebastian Peake 1989

Typeset in ITC New Baskerville by Origination, Dunstable.
Design by Forest Publication Services, Luton.
Cover design by Pocknell & Co.

Reproduced, printed and bound in Great Britain
by Butler and Tanner Limited, Frome and London.

For most of my life, I have had the omni-present influence of Mervyn Peake as poet, playwright, illustrator and writer all about me, physically and metaphysically. In writing A CHILD OF BLISS, I have tried to give tangible examples of my father as a man, not just as I have always held him to be, superman.

Work freely and madly and you will make progress
– Paul Gauguin

The aims of life are the best defence against death
– Primo Levi

CONTENTS

PHOTOGRAPHS

PROLOGUE

The intense love that I have had for my parents, with its resultant anguish and emotional ramifications, lives on for me. Although my father died in 1968 and my mother in 1983, the all-pervading atmosphere of their influence still envelops me, like a wonderful but harmless leprosy. I wish they would go away sometimes and leave me alone. Their own glamorous early life together, like a dream idyll, was something from which I felt totally excluded, and the frequent violent attacks I made on my father as a child and as a youth, swinging my fists and grappling him to the floor, were just the physical manifestations of my profound jealousy.

Throughout my life, my parents have had the greatest effect upon me. Wherever I was, I would write to them, whether as a child at school (as this book will show) or later, as an adult. My letters and cards were a varied lot, but I later discovered that they had been kept, a discovery that meant much to me. Their letters to me I kept, too.

My mother's collection of my correspondence included postcards and letters, notes from all over Europe, written as a young adult during the four years I lived and worked there, and during my trips to Africa and America, the Middle East and every part of the British Isles. My father wrote very infrequently. One of his rare letter shows his parental concern. After the disaster of my 'formal education', after failing all my GCE exams at the third attempt, he wrote a letter to me, just before I left the tutorial establishment in St Marychurch, near Torquay, where I was studying in 1957.

He begins with an experience that I had told him

about, when I had gone to see a great friend of mine in Jersey during the previous holiday, and had had the door shut in my face by the friend's mother. Oliver's father was at the time a minister in the French Government and was very unhappy about his son's academic progress. He and I shared the same tutors and they felt my influence to blame for the state of affairs, hence the mother's reaction. Though this was not an easy letter for me, my father went on to write to me as an equal, as one would to someone of the same age, using expressions like 'one can feel rather a "nut" if one is shut out'.

He continued:

...When you get home I am anxious that no time is wasted in regard to your work. We may not have your English results but in the meanwhile, while waiting for them, we must work out the best kind of plan for your future. You have so much to catch up on. The Allan experiment [Torquay tutors] was a ghastly and expensive failure. I can feel in your letter through what you say and how you say it, that you are reaching a stage that is more adult and interesting. Conquer your temper and you can become a most interesting and attractive chap. Make up your mind that you are a real student of life -

You have some fine qualities and I am often most happy about you. But then there are other times when you give way to another kind of mood. Also you have been really bad over such things as "forgetting" your Geography exam. That was a blow.

He went on to write that my mother had had a bad attack of laryngitis, and asked me to say when I'd be returning home.

He concluded:

We all send our love and hope you are happy. This letter
is not supposed to be a lecture, but I think it best to say
what is on my mind. Love

from Dad

That letter may not convey much of Mervyn Peake the artist, but Mervyn Peake the father is there. The father of a son whose life must have perplexed, worried and occasionally hurt the father. My memories of growing up as his son will show, I believe, that he had cause for concern, and at the same time, how much he mattered to me.

Another letter that it is fitting to quote now arose from a very different and terrible set of circumstances. After the onset of the awful diseases from which he suffered and subsequently died, he was sent for electrical shock treatment to an institution in Virginia Water, and in many heart-rending letters to my mother, pleaded for these experiences to stop. Not only in physical, but terrible mental pain, he cried out in these letters for the horror of Parkinson's Disease and encephalitis to be cured. Yet in 1963 he found time to write to me, and said in the note:

SEB

Dear Sebby: Just a note to thank you for your letter &
your news. I miss you also - old chap, and long to see you all
again. My longing is to sit in our sitting room, or in the
garden - the 5 of us all together.

I am most interested about the (Van 1940) and how you drove it from Wimbledon.

> *How is your drawing. <u>That</u>, I look forward to - too.*

I miss my father greatly, for he was an artist with unparalleled talents in many fields of the arts, and not only that, for he was also a man with a fine sense of humour who loved practical jokes; he played the mandolin and recorder well; he was an athlete - his high jump record at his public school remained unbroken for 25 years; he could belch from A to Z in one breath; speak Chinese; ride across La Coupee in Sark on his bike before the Germans built the concrete and railing bridge, with one foot on the saddle and one on the handlebars; he could paint, draw, and illustrate. And he could write, philosophically and with understated ease of the conflict between nature and man, these words:

> To live at all is miracle enough
> the doom of nations is another thing
> Here in my hammering blood pulse is my proof
> Let every painter and poet sing
> And all the sons of music ply their trade
> Machines are weaker than a beetle's wing
>
> Flung out of sunlight into Cosmic shade
> Come what come may the imagination's heart
> is constellation high and can't be weighed
>
> Nor greed nor fear can tear our faith apart
> When every heart-beat hammers over the proof
> That life itself is miracle enough.

I will begin my story overleaf. The illustration of despair that it sometimes provides was based on my craving for moments of familial happiness to continue unaltered, with me secure within the family. I always had with me, however far from my family, the memory of my mother's breast, of my father's stories, and the <u>feel</u> of home, which gave me an inimitable, poignant, indefinable sense of one's own private corner of love, kept alone for oneself, that secret thing.

CHAPTER 1

HAMLET
AND VILLAGES IN
SUSSEX-BY-THE-SEA

– Arundel Castle and the languid Arun

My life began in Littlehampton in Sussex, on the seventh of January, 1940 at three fifty in the morning, in the company of my paternal grandfather, who was a doctor, and a nurse. "It's a boy, Maeve", is the first recorded remark made about me, made by my grandfather who delivered me. Later, he planted a tree in his garden to commemorate my birth. Apparently I was a healthy boy with no birth marks. I cried a lot. I was in the nursing home for three days and my father, Mervyn Peake, brought me home. He had been told to stay away from the birth itself, because of his habit of fainting when confronted with anything slightly medical.

This first house which I lived in for some six months, was in a hamlet called Lower Warningcamp, near Arundel in Sussex, so-called because the Romans built lookout towers and encampments there. My parents had moved from Maida Vale from a fear of air-raids several months before I was born. Of this period, I remember nothing except those flashing, dream-like sequences when you think you remember things, but which are only the retrospective memories of hindsight, deceptions created by current reassessments of what you **feel** your earliest life was like. During the first few months of my life, my father worked on *Titus Groan*, but of course I knew nothing about it.

If I am aware of anything in the first year or so, it is the beautiful woman who looked down at me when I was being fed. Breast-fed by my mother, I was put to bed in a small bedroom but always slept badly. My father was so often away in the army, and it saddened my mother that my first tooth, and so on, were experiences shared only by post. Soon after we moved again, one of the many uprootings that punctuated my childhood. This move was to nearby Burpham where my grandfather lived. My parents took a flint cottage adjacent to his, a fourteenth-century group of tiny buildings later converted into one dwelling. Even then the place was still quite small, but since for some while only my mother and I lived there, there was enough room for us, though as a painter and sculptress my mother had her works all around the house, together with my father's paintings. It was a house with art stored in every room.

Whilst my father was away in the army, my mother would take me to Arundel once a week, on the back of her bicycle, and I travelled in a small metal seat just under the saddle. The three miles from the cottage were flat except for one or two small hills, but with the shopping done, the return journey was more difficult. I was left in the small seat all the time, and if I try hard, I can feel the wobbling of the frame of the bike as the shopping at one end in a basket and me at the other made the going quite hard for her.

It was at the age of two that I was no longer alone: my brother Fabian was born. In the summer of 1942 the sun shone in that way that people always seem to remember of their own youth and childhood, and from those summer mornings I can still hear the chirruping of the birds just outside my window. Rays of sunlight warmed up the bedroom and lit up my toys in the early mornings. These were my intimate toys, which then seemed so peculiarly one's own, but are often so ordinary and unoriginal when seen in later life.

My first memories of my father date from this time. He was still in the army and working on illustrated books - *The Rime of the Ancient Mariner* was one. I can see him now, as he takes off his army cap and puts his arms around my mother's waist. Then he would put his cap on my head. Except for the promotion to Captain made in order to facilitate his freedom of movement in Germany in the weeks

Baby, 1940

just after the War, my father was a sapper throughout his years in the army. As I grew up, with an awareness of the absence of my father around me, he was working, on rare moments of leave, on *Titus Groan*. When he came home to Burpham I was about three and a half, and as he came into sight just over the brow of the chalk sided road and down the few hundred yards leading to our cottage, his cap was my target. Somehow, although the whole man was my father, it was his cap that made me like him. I am sure he could easily have taken it off earlier, rules notwithstanding, but I must have shown such visible happiness the first time he placed it on my head, tipping it back so it almost drowned my skull, that on every subsequent and appropriately expectant moment he did the same. It could not have been a more ordinary thing, but he seemed a general, this private. He had made me a marvellous car, for even from the earliest age cars were a delight for me, a fact he rapidly realised. I would zoom down the garden path with his cap on my head in my grey bullet car and encircle my parents.

From this earliest point in my memory of my father, when the prisms of talented light, talented shade, and talented dark that coloured his life worked their magic into my consciousness, beaches, in their emptiness the opposite of the complicated artistic horizons that were his, played the fullest of parts. From Burpham the windy road to Littlehampton would be about five miles. When he came on leave, my parents and I would ride to the coast, me sitting in a basket over the front wheel of his bike or behind the saddle of hers, and I would sense the wobbling of the frame with wonder. My mother's bike had been bought by my father as a surprise when he had left her at the end of a leave. She loved it. En route to the beach, powered it seemed by the force of love and dependence, the bicycles would at first sail down the initial little hill, over which I had earlier seen the cap approaching, and I would hear the woosh of air in my mother's golden hair, stretched out in the wind and following two feet behind her head. There were smells of cows, smells of fields, the murky, dank smell of the River Arun and its adjacent meadows, reeds and grass. We sailed by towards the harder bit of the journey, the main south coast road. We only had to travel the very short distance between the evocative Arundel Station, with its awful, poignant partings and blissful arrivals, and the Littlehampton turn, opposite a convent. From the main road the road was fairly flat and sometimes my parents would have a race. There were only very occasionally vehicles of any kind; a slow, horse pulled hay cart in summer, or an old tractor whose driver would greet the passing cyclists and their little passenger, with the open, uncluttered greeting of an earlier way of life.

Now we came to a cluster of houses. This hamlet, Lyminster, was soon past, then over the level crossing and a half mile or so later, there was the seaside town of Littlehampton. If they had ridden enough and my little legs, folded up for the last four or five miles, had long since gone to sleep, they would drive straight to the beach, another half mile or so. If both parties, pushers and charge, could face it, they would turn right at the shops, past the railway station, over the bridge across the mouth of the Arun, and ride along the banks of the river to where it joined the sea. There were rolling dunes which stretched as far as the eye could see on the shore side and merged into the horizon beyond Climping. Out of my wickerwork cage, with its soporific effect on my legs and knees, I would hobble like a new-born fawn and gradually increase my strength before wildly tearing off along this long, open nothingness of golden sand which seemed limitless to me. I used to like pretending I was lost or abandoned, forgotten. Off I'd fly, my legs weaving out, with the beat of the heart, and the knowledge of my parents' **thereness**, away to a further point of the beach by the river. I knew that they would always wait for me, and that I would always come back.

This was where I learnt 'skimmy', at which my father was very adept. On still days he would pick up stones, for at

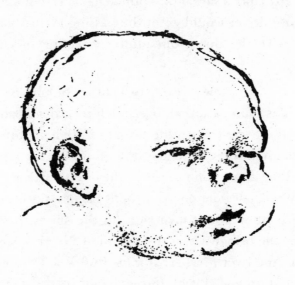

Baby, 1940

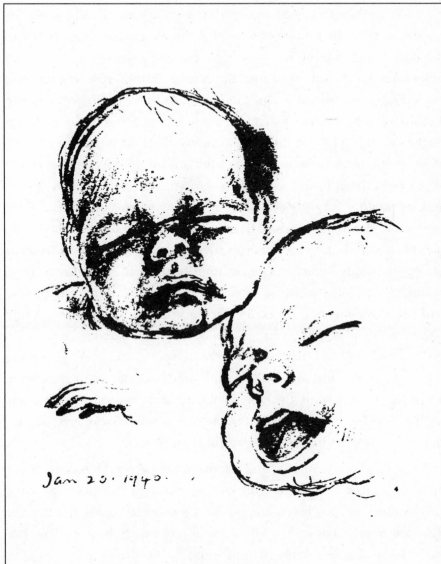

Jan 20. 1940.

Artist's son, 1940

high tide the beach is stony, and selecting them meticulously, would let the stones skim the surface of the water. He taught me the selecting of the best stones, not too heavy or light, flat like a doubloon. He could sometimes count up to twenty five times as they rose slightly and landed again on the surface of the water. At first I could only manage a plonk or two, my arm inadequate for the bent aim and the powerful throw needed. Little by little as I grew up I found I could skim as well as he could, but my record still lags behind his. Sometimes we would all go right down to the sea, a long way from the bicycles and clothes and we would sit in the pools and make great scarves of seaweed, dark brown and damp, like massive flat tongues with odd holes in them. My parents would drape each other in these strange wet shapes and cover me up like a tiny Robinson Crusoe, imprisoned with weed on my head, around my shoulders, across my arms and legs. Here my father, who had made a collection of stones on the way down to the sea, would build a tower of stones for me to aim at with others that were to hand. When I had knocked them over, one of us would rebuild the tower and the next one aim and so on. We would sometimes stay on the beach the whole afternoon until the sea would advance towards us, the tide having turned. Then, slowly, we would shuffle backwards on our bottoms, trying to be more successful than Canute.

At the end of the day, we would bicycle home along the river beside the golf course, through the town, past the railway crossing, and how I longed for the express to pass, but it never did. We returned down the hill, at the top of which the great fairy tale castle loomed above Arundel, and home to Burpham.

The beautiful flint walls of Sussex, especially the one surrounding our cottage in Burpham, or the one round my grandfather's house in the same village, played a part in our lives, as they were solid things, strangely shaped silver grey stone erections meant to last. I sat on them daily and never slipped, because of the gritty concrete top, rounded and secure, and I would dangle my legs over the edge, being careful not to cut my bare legs on the jagged flints which jutted out from the wall proper.

There must have been awful farewells at the gate or the local station when my father went off again after just a few days. Bedtime was marvellous when my father was home because it meant his reading stories to me, my father who had one of the greatest imaginations possible. Of course, like many children at the time, I heard the Beatrix Potter evergreens read to me; but it was the classics that came alive through my father. My father loved *Treasure Island* especially, and as he could quote passages by heart, later, when I could read, I would test him. I would read the first word or two, 'Squire Trelawney, Dr. Livesey and the rest of these gentlemen...' and he would then go on and on, faultlessly, with the story for pages if I had wanted. My mother would stick to the text much more than my father. Sometimes, whatever he was reading, he would go off on flights of his imagination, unable to stop himself. So Peter Rabbit might start off in Mr. McGregor's garden, and would end up on the beach with lots of local Sark or Kent or Chelsea friends, frying sausages over a roaring fire; or he would set out on all kinds of marvellous wanderings that would be quite at a tangent to his usual life. My father would make me a sort of tent out of the sheets and blankets and I would be snuggled up in it listening to strange stories of exotically named pirates of the Spanish Main or the South Seas or Jamaica, and shiver with fright. These great wild men, scabbards dangling to the ground, trailing sabres of blood-curdling sharpness, knives and blunderbusses, pistols and arms of all sorts, stalked my bedroom long after he'd said goodnight. With the wind sometimes outside howling, I imagined the voices of Blind Pew or his own Captain Slaughterboard, about whom C.S. Lewis wrote, in a letter to my father: 'How many parents have received doctors' bills for these children's disturbance I will never know, but other children's books pale into insignificance compared with yours.' I grew up knowing traditional bedtime stories very well, but interwoven with unique, strange and sometimes mad episodes: always exciting, always original.

The earliest sounds in life that one remembers are contained in a shroud of mist from which only slowly does the prosaic meaning emerge. An early dawn sound was the clink of the milk bottles arriving at the front doorstep, then mumbling in the next room, muffled sounds, unclear. In Burpham when my father was away in the army and before my brother was born, and even until he was a year or two old, I would open my eyes slowly on sunny days as the light advanced and hear the bird outside. Now that sound remains in my mind, the bird on a particular branch. From its perch, and of course there must have been many of them, it directed me by its call to the day coming. My reveille. Then about 7.30 a.m. or a little later, my mother would creep in and ask if I would like to 'climb in' with her. When my father was on leave, I would join them both and cuddle up in the middle and be in the deepest sea of contentment imaginable. I would mention my bird and we would listen for it. It would sing and when I was old enough, I would say that it was my 'early friend' and, like my Dinky toy cars, lined up so I could see them on waking along the window ledge, its sound has lasted my lifetime.

My father loved practical jokes. Later in the war, we lived for a short while in a billet in Blackpool. One morning my parents, together for the weekend as he was stationed nearby, awoke to find a huge wardrobe falling towards them and were unable to prevent its crashing down onto the floor. On lifting it up again, they watched as I calmly stepped out through the open door: I'd gone in unawares and not being able to get out, I pushed forwards against the door, causing it to fall. During this very weekend after I was asleep, they were to entertain a friend in the dining room. They were to meet downstairs and my mother, who was to follow my father downstairs after getting me to sleep - there were no cots and so I was put in the bottom drawer of the chest of drawers with a sheet and blankets covering me - was to come down a few minutes later. Meanwhile my father, wanting to play a trick on the other two, and remembering my activities, got into a large linen cupboard in the dining room while no-one else was there, and awaited their arrival. At last he heard sounds of chairs being pulled back and people sitting down, at which he sprang out making wild, monkey-like sounds, all the while sticking out his tongue. It was, however, two very shocked old ladies who saw this mad apparition leaping from the sideboard, and after they had somewhat composed themselves, he apologized by saying that he thought that they had been his wife and his best friend. As there was no-one else in the dining room, he only added to his apparent madness.

In the main, my early years were spent in Sussex. With the real possibility of a German invasion, the famous pitchfork and sickle brigades of the Home Guard proliferated, but it was the coming of the American Army down to the Sussex coast that gave us a greater sense of security than the old boys could, however noble their spirit. On most days, platoons would march past and often I would be sitting on the flint wall watching them, held by my mother. She was not only very attractive but always dressed with an idiosyncratic taste that caused her to be noticed, especially by homesick soldiers. One day an American soldier broke ranks and from behind his back gave my mother two pairs of black silk stockings, and gave me one of the most memorable gifts of my life. This was a khaki coloured Scout car, with moving gun turrets and lovely fat, round rubber sand tyres. This present, which I played with all the time, racing it up and along, over and under everything that had a surface, was my pride and joy and its loss in a move caused me real and unmitigated anguish which lasted for years.

Sadly, we never saw that soldier again for soon after we left the area, evacuated from danger. In those summer days before evacuation, the village hummed with sounds of agelessness, the church bell, the birds swooping and singing, the cattle on the surrounding hills, all the peace and tranquility of English village life. My brother and I had our evening bath outside in the long zinc tub. We had no inside bathroom or electricity: just a cold water tap. The bath would be filled and refilled and we'd splash naked in and out on the grass. I'd zoom my scout car around the edge of the bath and my little brother of one would gurgle, splash and shriek. My grandfather's house, just adjacent, built in the 1920's, had a sweeping drive to the front door through a little avenue of lilac and lavender bushes, the smell of which lingers in my memory. Some time after he retired (from the medical missionary service to different foreign missions and compounds in Tien'tsin, Peking, Kuling and Hangchow and different parts of China), a fire damaged the house: the roof was burnt and much of the house as well, since the roof was made of Reed Thatch. The red tiled roof that replaced it was an attractive enough substitute, but it was not the roof but the doctor's surgery that was most fascinating to me. In the hospital that he had built in Tien'tsin for cataract patients, he had kept photographs of all the awful afflictions that his patients suffered. These he kept still, and some were quite horrific. It took a strong stomach to see these medical records. He also had a five pound gallstone that he had removed from a dying Chinese patient, which is still used as a paperweight somewhere in the family. I wonder how these must have affected my father and his growing imagination.

The beauty of the shapes in chalk on the Downs, the myriad different forms in the flint rock, constitute much of this earliest part of my consciousness, as well as the Arun river, which was nearly the cause of my end before I'd quite begun. One day, my parents had hired a rowing boat and had set off, with Fabian and me, on a gloriously sunny afternoon during a weekend's leave. After rowing for half an hour or so upstream, my father decided that he wanted to take a photograph of his sons. He asked me to step onto the boat's rear seat, which I did, and as he left his seat to get a better angle from which to take the photo, I fell into the river. The Arun is particularly fast running, and although my father dived straight in after me, being fully clothed he could not really swim, but could only flail and wallow hopelessly. I can still hear the gurgling of the water as it swept me away and as I started to lose consciousness. Tragedy beckoned: during the whole afternoon when they had in turn floated and oared their way along the river, they had neither met nor seen anyone else. Then, as their panic reached its height, for I was presumed lost, two professional scullers came swiftly round the bend in the river and seeing the confusion, dived in and I was saved. I had to be given respiratory attention to regain consciousness, but I survived because of those masters of timing.

Sometimes my parents would go for walks together. When they did, and I accompanied them, pushed as a small child, later holding hands and running and skipping beside them, there was always fun with stones or twigs, branches or boughs. Using a stick as a kind of golf club my father would make small, round, stones scurry off along the lane for me to chase after and retrieve. He would bend twigs supply into strange shapes or choosing fallen branches in autumn, after storms or high winds, would put the V of the branch up above his forehead and say that he was a stag - a wild one, and would come after me or my mother, baying and whinneying. He told me a story once on one of these walks, when I was perhaps seven or eight, about the appalling end that befell enemies of certain North American Indian tribes, whereby the outstretched legs of the victim were strapped to either branch of a taut, forked bough. The rope holding back their captive was cut, the branches would fly apart, and the victim would then be ripped in half. When walking along cliffs, my father would sometimes pretend to slip at the very edge of a precipice and scare my mother senseless, then spring back on to the path unharmed.

When we lived in Sussex, one of their favourites was The Lepers' Path. They would often keep to the route taken by my grandfather who had shown them it originally. It snaked along the lee of the South Downs and from afar looked like a white knife wound which had gouged out a path from the grass that covered the chalk. They would talk of his work, his book, paintings, drawings, his poems, his plays, and invent wonderful names together that would be added to the short lists they regularly made, of candidates for inclusion in his works. On these walks Flay, Swelter, Prunesquallor, and other exotic, idiosyncratic onomatopoeic names were invented for my father's characters. They would try out sounds to see if they suited the characters' nature, and jettison hundreds in the process. They would arrive back at the Burpham cottage exhausted from imaginings, but with a dossier of new ideas for my father to work on.

When my brother and I would go off to the beaches on summer days, we would run ahead of our parents, whom we would ask to follow on, five minutes later. On Sark, there were no motorized vehicles except the rare tractor. We could tear down the middle of any of the roads and not worry about anything. Usually we would race as fast as possible up to the windmill and hide inside. They would then either walk past or ride past, and by the slight raising of their voices in feigned pretence that they didn't know where we were, we would jump out shrieking, "Here we are, you didn't know we were here, did you?!"

On his way back overland from China when he was eleven years old, my father had got off the Trans Siberian Express at Omsk, where the station was some way outside the town. It was mid-winter and the landscape was pure white. Snow covered everything, even the line, before the snow plough attached to the front of the two engines had cleared a path. He had been expressly asked by his parents not to leave the train, but had climbed down from the carriage because he wanted to feel the snow. As he was only a small boy and the carriage being very far above the ground, there was a big jump from the lowest stepping board onto the snow below. Not only was this deep, but the temperature very much below zero, and the approaching darkness of late afternoon all made this exploit very dangerous. All he wanted to do was to play in the snow, unaware that the train was taking on water from the tower which was situated some way from the station proper. The train having filled up with the required amount of water, a great hissing and opening up of the boilers took place, and the great long express from Vladivostok to Paris started very slowly to move forward. My grandparents had by now noticed my father's disappearance from their compartment and had sent for the guard to help them find him. Although the train had begun to move and my father was still several feet below the still open carriage door, Dr. Peake could, by holding onto one of the handles at the side of the door, ease his free hand down far enough to grab his son. By now my father was running alongside the train in the snow, but was pulled to safety and back into the train. This story of his getting off the train in Siberian mid-winter was always used, by my parents, as the tale *par excellence* of what would have happened, **if**...?

Several years later when we lived at Smarden in Kent, my father, brother and I would go sometimes to the level crossing in Headcorn, a town nearby, and would watch the expresses rush by, with their steam whistles and pure grace as they thundered past, making the earth tremble and vibrate with their power and speed. This reminds me of *Gormenghast*, though the 'Thing' that features throughout the book is not necessarily anything mechanical; it could be fleeting love or an eagle, a rocket or that beautiful moment in life when for a tiny space of time one fools oneself into believing that transsubstantiation is understandable. The Mallard engine was like that, as it flew past at 100 m.p.h.; beautiful and shaped like the most perfect of bullets that could shoot dead straight into eternity. This exotic and powerful engine, pulling prosaic-looking carriages behind it, was only seen once at our level crossing vantage point, but it left a mark in all our imaginations that lasted long, long after its last tiny carriage had disappeared into the distance of mid-Kent.

Travelling on trains with me involved my parents with a child that seemed permanently to be screaming. Once, during a journey which lasted 17 hours, I allegedly screamed from when the train set off from Arundel Station all the way to Blackpool. This journey involved several changes and during the last long, slow part I was comforted by a soldier who could see the weariness in my mother, and putting me on his knee sang songs for hours while the blacked-out train ambled at snail's pace towards Lancashire. When my parents were first engaged and wanting privacy, my father would do a drawing of a totally authentic looking madman sticking his tongue out and making a wild face. If anyone looked as though they wanted to join them in the compartment he would place this drawing against the window. Apparently it always worked, for even if the drawing didn't do the trick, the fact that the person holding it to the window had gone to such lengths to keep others at bay was taken to imply the same state of mind as the figure depicted.

Before I was born, my father travelled for more than a year up and down daily between Wallington and Victoria after he'd got a job teaching at the Royal Academy School, and would practice his craft of drawing on the crowded trains. At that time, the early 1930's, most businessmen still wore the bowler hat and striped dark suit, and Wallington was the very essence of *petit bourgeois* sobriety. But people didn't mind being drawn, and would often ask him if they could keep the results. In this way, many hundreds of his studies of people 'caught', as my mother noted in her book, in the act of living, were given away. These drawings, now sometimes fetching thousands of pounds each, are a regular feature of fine art sales, and in several instances form little collections – hoarded and put up for sale decades later.

Only occasionally did I express myself through the art chosen by my parents. When I was fifteen I gave my mother a pen and ink drawing of myself that she kept in the hall with the other paintings and drawings. This drawing captured, I'm told, the downward angle of my face and the sense of loneliness that seemed to emanate from me, which I have tried to expunge from my being. It always seems to return, like a wrinkled old person's lines which partly disappear when they roar with laughter, only for the deep lines of age to return. Sometimes I would grin broadly for long periods to force my face to look happy or lighthearted, but the skin would seem to force the natural shape back to the image that comes over in this drawing.

When I was about seven years old, I produced three watercolours for my parents – all were quite large, about three feet by two feet. One was of strange beasts at sea, a great sailing ship with flying pigs and baboons, long necked giraffe-like animals cavorting in the heinous currents, and I think I was seen as a sort of potential prodigy. The second was of a gypsy washerwoman in scarves, hanging up her washing on a line with a tiny, dwarflike apparition at her side; and the third equally bizarre, with bounding figures wildly floating and darting in space about the Earth. All three pictures were framed and placed in my parents' bedrooms in every house we lived in, for they were done especially for them and I think they really loved this present from me. A sort of self portrait figures in one corner of one of these three pictures, where a small child appears to be floating above the choppy blue sea and is obviously loving the abstract world around it. As they were executed when I was so young and as I did no more work in the conventional art sense, painting or drawing, for the next eight or ten years, these three pictures meant a lot to my mother. But they were efforts that had no predecessors as yardsticks against which to judge progress and, for a decade, no successors.

Nevertheless, if I created few works of art, I figured in many. Portraits of children were ubiquitous in the Peake household. Every wall had paintings or drawings on them – of myself, Fabian, or later our sister Clare, cousins, even children of friends. These drawings, some in the fine, dextrous line of pencil, some

As Jim in Treasure Island – *overhearing the murderous plot.*

gouache, some water colour, all brought to their subjects life, held in that second of play or concentration that my father would see, catch and put down. Sometimes a canvas was placed on an easel and I would pose for long periods. There would be breaks, when he would say, 'You can have a rest' from the prone position I was in, and these would be enough for him to get back into the mood for another quarter- or half-hour session, when, behind the canvas, the unseen energy was again applied to the new work. Finally, he would emerge and I would be allowed to rest and 'have a look' at myself as Jim in *Treasure Island*, a Dickens urchin or a character from *Swiss Family Robinson*.

• • •

I was drawn, painted, sketched and 'gouache'd' many, many times, and I always loved the results. I became a leaping athletic hero with pistols in both hands up the rigging in the 'Hispaniola', or hiding in an apple barrel listening to the murderous plot nearby. My mother would read the book being illustrated at the time and my father would paint or draw, while I stood, or sat at the pine table, sometimes in costume, sometimes naked, sometimes dagger or sword in hand, but always in action of one sort or another.

He drew me many times as I was about to go back to the detested boarding school, and always caught that look or glance that was my mood at the time. I have so many of these drawings and paintings and I can go back to the room, the atmosphere and time when they were done. I can relive the smell and feel of the occasion, its uniqueness, and although I didn't know it, the sheer power of these images taken from the written word and put so powerfully on paper. I can't say that I always relished the idea of posing as much as I did, but in the main the atmosphere was workmanlike and easy, almost as though I was an apprentice to my father's wishes.

There would always be picture frames around the house. There was a collection of discarded ones, found at the Royal College or Central Schools, Chelsea or the Slade, old, often rather tatty, hardly ever new. New frames came much later and not until the mid-1960's did the famous Sark fishermen series of the mid-1930's, or any of the subsequent oils have decent frames. The many thousands of drawings were kept in a specially made artist's drawers. These drawers, very shallow but quite deep, held his most beautiful illustrations. The *Ancient Mariner* drawings, commissioned by Chatto and Windus and for which he received £10 and now valued in excess of £10,000 each; the drawings for *Treasure Island, Bleak House, Quest for Sita, The Hunting of the Snark,* all were kept in this unusual cabinet and followed us in all our moves. Many of his oil paintings are still unframed. Hundreds of drawings also remain in their original protective wrappers, as he was simply so prolific. After his death in 1968 my mother spent what was then a large amount of money framing 30 or 40 major oils and several hundred drawings, illustrations and water colours, bringing them to even greater life. I remember a marvellous game once, where he and I skipped and danced through the Sark house, him with a large wooden frame, and me with a smaller one resting on our right shoulder, being held in place by our right hand, and hopping from one side of the lower part of the frame to the other, with our feet sometimes on the inside and then on the outer sides of the frame. Making wild Red Indian whoops, we went upstairs and down, out into the garden, round the duck pond and in and out of the bunker until we had had enough. Once my father put the front cover of a *Picture Post* magazine into a frame under glass. It showed a beautiful girl, but he blacked out a tooth or two, then took it to show the vicar's wife who greatly admired my father's talents. He had 'touched up' this beauty so well that the photo appeared to be an oil, and her apparent need of a dentist was so convincing that the vicar's wife couldn't understand why his subject had let my father paint her with her mouth open.

Pencils were everywhere, in tins or jars, boxes or drawers.   Especially prevalent were the 3B kind, soft and supple, giving smooth, full lines. I remember hearing sharpening of pencils long before I knew what it meant: a kind of tiny scraping, clipping sound that came out of the workrooms - it was **his** sound. Later, when more aware of his craft and the utensils used, I would watch quietly while he would take the used pencils out of their receptacles, sharpen each one and put them all back, base first, into the jam jars, ready for use. He must have had hundreds. Not as many as fountain pens, however, which he lost frequently. My mother would replace the pens, usually good ones, Shaeffer, Parker, Conway Stewart or Watermans, and when she could afford it, gold ones which he loved. I remember once hearing her say, "But Mervyn, that is the seventeenth gold pen you've lost. Couldn't you look after them better, darling, and not lose them?"

CHAPTER 2

CHELSEA IN THE DAYS OF THE ARTISTS

– Dylan Thomas sometimes takes me to kindergarten

At the end of the war, in 1944, we moved to Chelsea. From this time there is a well known story in the family, one retold in my mother's book on her life with my father, *A World Away*, of the lions which, my brother was convinced, were looking at him from behind the curtains at his window. It began, his conviction, at the same time as a private vendetta against my parents by a fanatic who lived nearby in Chelsea, who had taken a real dislike to one of my father's paintings. Disturbing incidents had happened and these took place just outside my brother's bedroom. One night my parents had Graham Greene in for the evening, and they played a game of practical tricks in which people's names were picked out from the telephone directories, who were then telephoned to be the unfortunate recipients of their wit. Suddenly, a terrifying scream went up, emanating from Fabian's room. He had seen lions and they were coming for him, he was sure. He was so beside himself with fear that the practical jokes were abandoned and my mother stayed for a long time with him, trying to calm him before he went back to sleep. They remained for years, these nightmares about the lions, and the family always felt that the *malfaiteuse* did actually do something involving strange costumes or masks outside his window, that he took for a pride of lions.

Our Chelsea house was a small Regency one painted charmingly, with a carved oak door and painted ceramic panels inset on the outside front wall. It was just off the King's Road. There was one main sitting room, a small kitchen off the main room and two small bedrooms above. At the time, 1945, my father was busy revising *Titus Groan*, one of his now famous books which he had begun in the Army and was due for publication later the same year. Peter Ustinov lived almost next door, Carol Reed next to him, and in a building across the road, Augustus John had a studio. I used to go to visit the painter sometimes with both my parents, sometimes just my father. There was a lovely bread shop, which sold cakes and did cream teas, just yards from his studio entrance, and I can bring back vividly those pre-boutique days when the King's Road really had an atmosphere of artistic and literary activity about it. Dylan Thomas, a friend of the family, would sometimes hold my hand and take me to kindergarten at the end of the road, and one day *Picture Post* did a feature on it in their magazine, but to my childish annoyance my brother got into the piece and not me. A few days later, I ran away in the milk break, and on knocking at our front door a few hundred yards away and finding no-one in, I wandered about, finally being brought home by Dylan Thomas, on whose knee I sat outside our front door until my parents arrived home.

Dylan Thomas was not a very important part of my father's life, but one day in 1946, when asked to give a lecture at a fairly august institute in the West End, he asked my father if he could borrow one of his suits. My father obligingly lent him two to see which one fitted, but he never saw either again. One was of lovely brown corduroy, a style I've always liked myself, and to make up for the disappearance of his, I have had several in my time. They always remind me of that incident.

During a lull in the bombing, and after an all-clear signal had been given, my parents took me to the cinema in the King's Road. The Odeon, now a shop, was near the corner of Sydney Street, and I had passed it many times while being taken for walks. Once I was walking down the King's Road holding Dylan Thomas's hand and I had asked him if he would take me to the cinema. He refused in a very gentle way, the probable reason being a lack of funds, The Chelsea Potter or The Markham Arms having taken the last of his usually very meagre resources. On this day, however, I was taken, and inside what excitement! It was the first showing of *Dumbo*, the elephant who sails and gracefully glides around the air currents. I was enthralled by it: dreaming of Dumbo, talking of him, living it all over and over again. I had a special friend at this time, a cockney boy from a street or two away from where we were living. He heard about Dumbo so often from me, as we ran and dashed about the bomb craters near the embankment, that one day he failed to meet me at our usual rendezvous. I found out later that Dumbo had split us: he couldn't take my love for this sentimental Disney creature.

I would be taken sometimes to Peter Jones in Sloane Square where, in 1944, my father had an exhibition of paintings, to have tea in the restaurant on the fifth floor overlooking the trees in the Square below. I would always feel very proud of my attractive mother, elegant and quietly glamorous, with golden hair down to her waist, and hazel eyes. When as a joke my father or brother called them brown, she would feign pain and whisper that they were wasp gold. They were lovely and I got used at quite a young age to the daily glances and compliments she received.

On V.E. night I was taken – as a great treat – to see the lights, dancing, rejoicing and celebrations of that memorable day. We had a space on one of the benches booked for the family and we watched, cheered and clapped as all the army, navy, air force, nursing and bands of every regiment, colour and part of the Services marched past. Planes flew overhead, floodlights flashed and the evening finished with great moving tears as laughter-filled patriotic songs were sung.

CHAPTER 3

SARK C.I. –
A BOYHOOD IDYLL
ON A GRANITE ROCK

– Days of sun and stormy seas and sad, sad partings

Then in 1946 something happened that was very important in all our lives: we moved to Sark, in the Channel Islands. Moving was a frequent part of the Peakes' life. I lived with my parents, and latterly my mother, in nine different houses, flats, rooms or studios, but the moves seem to have been comparatively easy affairs because my parents had very few possessions. The table, a few chairs, a bookcase or two, that was about all. The main complication involved in any of the many moves was the number of paintings and drawings, since they were very precious and easily damaged. My trunk, with 'S. Peake' beautifully inscribed on it by my father, for my first time away from home, when I was sent away to school, would be used for my few possessions: my Dinky toy car collection, my clothes, shoes, books. This trunk, so much part of the lot of the child sent off to boarding school, I have still. Our moves were ordered, quiet affairs, because apart from the paintings, we had no Georgian tables or porcelain that could come to grief. What was of worth, not perhaps according to the accepted yardstick of inherited or purchased wealth, were those objects peculiar to the Peakes.

My father was not a great reader, but possessed many books, and one aspect of these many moves was the many tea chests, containing the hundreds of books that weighed a ton, as any remover will vouch. The bookcases, whether primitive structures of bricks and planks, or later, the usual wooden kind, contained many wonderful first editions. The magnificent *Don Quixote*, illustrated by Doré, that my parents were given, containing whole block plates etched in memorable black against the sombre dark quality of the

'Jim' in Treasure Island

writing, was the weight of 50 paperbacks.

Later some Pan paperbacks joined the hardback collection. My father had designed the pipe motif, and had to choose between the ten pounds offered for the drawing, or a royalty on each use of the design. At the time, during the war, paper was scarce and it was not thought that a paperback edition could be sustained. In the circumstances, my father followed the advice of a friend and took the flat fee. As there were about four 'Pans' on each book published and as it became an incredibly successful imprint, my father would have been rich indeed. Wisdom after the event.

Graham Greene sent my parents a copy of most of his books as they were published, often signed, and these formed and remain a very important part of my late parents' mutual collection. They were catholic in their taste, Dickens being a great favourite, as well as R.L. Stevenson, James Joyce, Flaubert and Zola. Books were all around me and I was taught early on the worth of books. My parents collected books for the pleasure of having them in the house and as a reminder of how they had been moved or influenced by the writing.

Apart from his own illustrated books, which I read or had read to me, my taste for literature until the age of 18 or so did tend to veer towards the easiest of forms. The adventures of Blyton's 'Five' held me in its summer of yesteryear atmosphere, tinged as it was with tolerable criminality at the edges. Apart from these, famous war books, *The White Rabbit*, *The Dam Busters*, *Colditz*, gripped me and I read every one, advancing my knowledge of other literature not one jot. The stuff of youth, easy, prosaic, but so exciting at the time. My god-father gave me a leather bound copy of *The Forsyte Saga* on my twelfth birthday, a kind, well meant and surely perceptive gift. It remains in its virgin state today. If only I had had the brains to see that Thackeray and Blyton can both be devoured, not one or the other; the easy 'other' being my route. I gave myself a crash course in reading to replace my literary ignorance from about 18 onwards, and read Chekhov, Pushkin,

Tolstoy, Gogol and Dostoyevsky like a man possessed, day and night and at every opportunity, followed by my favourite Americans: Faulkener, Thomas Wolfe, Walt Waltman, all of Salinger, twice, all of F. Scott Fitzgerald, and in the easiness of its fine popular writing, Steinbeck. I hope this was due to my parent's influence.

Graham Greene I loved, his travels not only with his aunt, his alcoholic priests, his crooks and tarts, but most of all the sweating descriptive powers of Africa and Central America. Later I admired Heinrich Boll, Thomas Mann, Gunther Grass and that wonderful poet and perceptive human Heinrich Heine. All these so different, but all so powerful in atmosphere. What would life have been like without them? Surely far emptier? Many of these were presents from my parents. I was not asked to read by my father or mother. All that was ever done was suggesting that I might 'find something' in such and such a writer. How right they were to choose that path for me, initially to smile gracefully or accept the recommendation knowing I wouldn't probably do anything about it, but for it to have been obvious, later, that their choices were right Forcing me or ignoring me in the field of reading would not have led to the catholic love of, say, Marques, Borges, Baschevis Singer, Primo Levi or Anthony Burgess: favourites in my current world.

The abundance of books that my parents possessed made up in some way for a lack of other possessions. My parents' kitchens had no gadgets, except for a tin opener, and the Aga installed by the previous owner of one of their many houses. The scrubbed table, bought at a jumble sale for ten shillings in Sark in the mid-1940's, was the focal point of a very simple kitchen in whichever house one was in. A simple wooden draining board, a sideboard and much later a refrigerator, cutlery and some silver left to my mother on her parents' death were the accoutrements of family life, which as in so many houses took place around mother's kitchen.

The kitchen revolved round the table and chairs

and the talk there was of artists, of shape and form, of light and shade, of colour, of personality. Would you save the cat or a Rembrandt if a fire broke out? My mother the cat, my father the painting. And for me too, the choice of the painting, for me the 'living' masterpiece. This luxurious and hypothetically inane question exercised my mind many times. The scrubbed pine table, white from a thousand scrubbings, was used from the distance of my earliest memory until just before my mother's death four decades later. The legs that wobbled, the grooves in the top where the wood was worn down, the uneven opening of the drawers at either end, the personality of it, the thousand meals had on it, even its ignorance of its part in a family history took it far above the dignity of a noble Sheraton. There was no sophistication to it, no style, nothing beyond utilitarian, but it was unique and wonderful.

My mother had a penchant for simple earthenware vases rather like a pitcher, which could have been used for milk or water or, in Latin countries, wine. Brown, with a yellowish rim, these vases, of which there were several, always contained my mother's favourite daffodils or lilies. In the Spring and early Summer when the car-free lanes of Sark would be teeming with buzzing life and the hedgerows came out of hibernation and into a thousand stirrings of green, we would dash along the stone lanes and pick wild flowers to take home, and in the Autumn hunt blackberries for jam or wolfing there and then. The house would then be alive with the smells we had brought back and the wafting of the golden and yellow and white daffodils would be everywhere. They are now my favourites, and when they are placed around the room, I can shut my eyes and feel Sark again.

Breakfast with my parents was always boiled eggs, doorstep fried bread and 'Post Toasties', my father's word for any cereal, which derived from his boyhood in China. He, his brother and their parents lived for a while in the American compound in Kuling, and an American who also lived there always ate a brand, unknown to us, called Post Toasties. My father took a great liking to them and forever afterwards called cornflakes Post Toasties, Weetabix Post Toasties, even porridge Post Toasties.

My father was not much of an eater, but he loved everything my mother made and always complimented her on her efforts. Breakfast, after the Post Toasties, meant great pieces of fried bread or toast – and when on Sark my father loved the appearance of butter, which came in moulds in the shape of buildings, giving impressions of Sark Castle or other edifices, usually the Dame's house, La Seignerie, or Le Manoir, a fine stone Georgian house nearby. This golden coloured butter set in the moulds and delivered to the individual customer's houses direct from the farms, was ladled out of the dish with sad sighs, as the lovely designs were scooped away. We all sat around the famous table eating toast and talking excitedly of local events or the forthcoming episode of what at the time held us all entranced, Dick Barton Special Agent. Then off to the local little tiny school - 'Smallest in Great Britain' - my mother and I would go, and my father if he was with us would go to his workroom to write, illustrate or paint. My mother would clear up – she was extremely tidy – and afterwards would go to her own room to paint.

The house we moved to on Sark had been the H.Q. of the occupying German forces and they had painted the place in a camouflaged grey, had taken away all features like balconies and porticoes and toolsheds and had made the place feel unlike any home. After my parents had acquired the house on a 99 year lease at £80 per annum, the place was painted white and all the features replaced. Our first night was one devoid of furniture, but paintings were, of course, everywhere.

I loved this house with its great garden, the small pond, in which we put the ducks given to my father by the local vicar as a quid pro quo for a drawing my father did for him, and an underground bunker the Germans had dug in the garden in case of invasion.

When we arrived, the Sark house still had signs in German on the doors, and all around were other signs of the occupation: there was the flooded bunker which we used for boating and catching frogs; there were the lookout posts, the rusted armaments, the evidence on the tree nearby, from which, according to unfounded local gossip, people had been hanged for alleged collaboration. All over the islands, for I knew them all very well later in life, were piquant reminders of the Germans. Yet there was something about this legacy, in its concrete form, that was attractive to me - its solidity. These relics are everywhere still – 50 years later. Their potential as hiding places and the games that we could play on top of, inside, and at the back of these shapeless monuments of power meant that they held a fascination for us. Not so the concentration camp. My father visited Belsen a few weeks after liberation, with the inmates all still in their huts, many dying of typhus. He drew them, spoke to them and wrote the most eloquent and moving poems about some of the dying that have ever been written. This one I cannot forget:

Belsen, 1945

If seeing her an hour before her last
Weak cough into all blackness I could yet
Be held by chalk-white walls, and by the great
Ash coloured bed,
And the pillows hardly creased
By the lightness of her little jerking head -
If such can be a painter's ecstasy,

(Her limbs like pipes, her head a porcelain skull)

Then where is mercy?

And what irony?

Is this my calling, for my schooled eyes see

The ghost of a great painting, line and hue

In this doomed girl of tallow?

O anguish! has the world so white a yellow

As the pernicious and transparent mist

That like a whiff of Belsen in her cheeks

Detaches her by but a breath from linen

In that congested and yet empty world

Of plaster, cotton and a little marl?

Than whiteness what is there more terrible?

There lay the gall

On the dead mouth of the world

And at death's centre a torn garden trembled

In which her eyes like great hearts of black water

Shone in their wells of bone,

Brimmed to the well-heads of the coughing girl,

Pleading through history in that white garden;

And very close, upon the small head's cheekbones,

As upon ridges in an icy dew

Burned the sharp roses.

My father's experiences in Belsen, a place set in the flat forest region of northern Germany, remained in his conscious and subconscious mind from that visit until he died. When the condemned war criminal Peter Back saw my father at the cell door, he jumped up and saluted my father, and after the sketches had been recorded, he saluted and said, "*Danke schon*". He was hanged some hours later, an event to which my father was invited to attend. The senior S.S. wardress had to be punched and kicked to make her stand for the British Officer taking my father around the camp. When he had drawn this woman, who had come with Rudolph Höss, last Commandant of Auschwitz, to complete the *Endlosung* of the Jews, she approached my father and spat all over his face before being thrown back onto her bunk. She was a murderess from the most awful place in history and her physical prowess made her quite capable of killing my father. In *Titus Alone* (which has a mood fundamentally different from *Titus Groan* and *Gormenghast*) the evil man Veil and the faceless millions staring expressionlessly from the windows in the factory are both testaments to his experience of Belsen.

Expunging complicated feelings of guilt about the way in which my father had accepted his visit to Belsen, when he could have turned away on being dropped at the gate on that dark day in 1945, was almost an obsession with me for over 20 years. When the extent of the atrocities became known to me, I read avidly anything I could on the subject. Borrowing books from the library, buying books, talking to people who had been incarcerated, all I felt I had to do to try to ameliorate in some distorted way the lot that I knew to be that of the inmates, and of my father visiting them, treading across the human excrement everywhere, seeing the S.S. guards pulling the skin and bones across the rough ground, hearing the skulls of the dead cracking on the stones, the shaking of the nearly dead in the communal pits; the heaps upon heaps of cadavers and the near skeletons and the vomiting by the former captors as they scraped bodies from the teeth of the bulldozers' scoops. How can his experience of the camp not have created an eternal helplessness of the soul?

I soon found out, however, that it is one thing to have been there, and to have lived in the atmosphere of total war, and quite another to be able to go to visit these places now: however well intentioned my visits were essentially an emotional kind of voyeurism. I feel very ambivalent about my father's work at Belsen because my admiration for his total genius does not excuse the circumstance of his visit. Is he the greater talent, still misunderstood by many who should be ashamed of their ignorance, because he suffered and later died as a result of seeing manifest the antithesis of joy, love and beauty, or is he the bigger for *Titus*, the *Ancient Mariner* drawings, the idiosyncratic depth of painful, intuitive and explosive observation? I don't know.

Between 25-30,000 died in Belsen, ten times that amount in Chelm and Sobibor. Even a small camp on the Baltic near Gdansk-Stutthof, with its meandering small gauge lines ending up in a clearing in a wood and the Alsatian dog house (the first building seen upon entering the compound) still intact, witnessed terrible numbers of deaths. Treblinka in Eastern Poland, is built a few feet above the marshes, with its pretend railway station and clock. Even more overwhelming is the massive and bloodcurdling Auschwitz. The scaffolds are still there, the wall against which many more were shot than died in Belsen, the never-ending lines of huts – making me feel as though the thousands upon thousands of shaved heads were looking down on me, the visitor. There one sees photographs taken just before the death march to the gas chamber. The newly canonised Maximilian Kolbe, who took the place of a gypsy family and died in their stead, was gassed in the chambers that now one can walk through.

I shook before I saw the dreadful name Oswiecim coming into view when I drove across Poland a few years ago. It was, I felt, as though I was walking where I had no place to be – and this before I even arrived in the town. In an article in a magazine I had seen the most chilling photograph of the rails leading up to the main entrance to Birkenau, the women's part of Auschwitz. It had been taken in an early morning mist, and the finality of that line and its entrance under the great black wooden tower, shook me completely. Years later, when I walked along that track deliberating at 6 a.m. on a freezing day, the death-like poignancy of the place was hideous, despite my being the only person in the whole camp.

I felt that I had to write my own poetry, capturing my own feelings about concentration camps.

Treblinka, Eastern Poland

On the eastern side of nowhere
twelve hundred miles from home
the marshes of the hinterland
obscure the Polish soil.

Reeds and wetlands are all there is to see
of the million souls that met their fate
passing under the hour still clock.

The 'transit' station, leading
nowhere, the facade that fooled the lot
now houses one lonely guide
in the 'station masters' hut.

Bergen-Belsen KZ

He'd seen her shattered smile
and put it down in ink.

I saw a heart rending look, but
from a photograph.

The silence of the heath, the proof
with mass graves.

The gypsies plaque and Belgium's pure
simplicity, 'Matria Belgiae'.

Ann Frank stared out at us as
Modern British soldiers cried:

The bastards!

Kramer from Auschwitz came, and others too,
to smash the weak, and feeble.

Or is it in all of us
that desire to destroy?

The Poles encourage visits by children and foreigners and I agree. I think in some ways we should be obliged to visit these places where the grossest of violent acts took place. In one camp though, some school-children came sauntering towards me, chewing gum, smoking and singing pop songs. I found it difficult to grasp their unawareness as they strolled around what was to them just another old boring museum. Walking in Treblinka I tripped, and, looking down at the skeleton of a hare, prostrate, staring up at me in its death state, I froze. At Chelm camp in central Poland, in a mile square clearing in the forest, all that remains is the electrified entrance gate stating that in the space of only 18 months, 300,000 people died, including tens of thousands of Czech children and old people. There was a woman arranging some paltry flowers at the stone mausoleum a couple of hundred yards into the camp, whom I asked for information.

She spoke no German, except a few words, and I spoke no Polish. French was no good either, so in a combination of sign language and her very elementary German, she explained that if I would like to kneel down she would show me something. I did so, and there just half an inch or so below the surface were the bones of some of the children buried. 25,000 were shot, gassed or knifed to death on their arrival and because the mass graves filled up so quickly and there were so many, the bodies just got higher and higher in the pits, until just the small amount of earth covered them. She put a selection of arm and leg bones into my hand and made the knifing gesture across her throat. I dropped the bones almost at once. I felt completely unclean touching them. This woman had lived in the camp for the entire period of its existence and was in charge of washing the clothes taken from the victims just before their death. Then those pathetic garments were bundled into sacks and taken by horse and cart to the railway station about three miles away and sent to Germany.

All these camps that I had felt compelled to visit had the same chilling feel to them, whether small, medium or large, in woods or hills or on marshes, in high ground or in valleys. Usually they are silent places and should be visited, for even empty and laid flat, grassed over as in many cases, they exert such a power that only those with no imagination could fail to be profoundly moved and embarrassed by mankind's evil.

• • •

Sark had at the time about 360 people, most of whom were indigenous, patois-speakers: "un shoulder de boeuf", "un leg de mouton" they would say in the butcher's. The strange and very pronounced, rather South African accent of Sark I have always loved, and recently I gave a lecture to a Californian audience in a Sarkese accent, as the subject of my talk was *Mr Pye*, one of my father's books written on and about Sark. My audience was baffled.

It was a splendid place to grow up in. In the high summer my mother would pack a lunch and we would go on various bicycles off to some of our favourite haunts: beaches, cliff tops, the lovely and dangerous Venus Pool on Little Sark with its dark depths invisible below the lure of its blue and shimmering surface.

In the mid-1930's, when my father lived on Sark in an artists' colony, breeding cormorants, painting like a man possessed and drawing until the lead had worn down to the fingers holding the pencil, he found a whale. At least he was told of the whale, which had been carried out of its normal path in the Atlantic, and had somehow become parted from its fellow travellers and landed up on Grand Greve beach. Very few local people liked the idea of going very near the putrifying remains of the grounded mammal, but my father, with handkerchief at nostrils, went to examine it. There were a few other brave souls prepared to go up to the carcass and between them they collected some of the whale's larger vertebrae as mementoes. These bones were dried out and scraped of all appended flesh and a small collection of them kept. Throughout their life together my parents treasured these beautifully shaped bones, which had so delighted my father. They travelled with us when we moved and now, long after my parents' death, they still grace the fireplaces or mantlepieces of my home and those of my brother and sister. Their shapes can be seen as a horse's head, a gargoyle, a ship, or strange flying objects, modern in the extreme and yet ancient like China, strange emblems of power. My father was fascinated by the idea of bones from a whale who lost its way in the great ocean and who ended its life on a beach in the Channel Islands, finally dismembered for the unique shapes formed along its back.

Bones had a perennial fascination for my father. He once bought a skull and many other bones from a museum which

1.
*With my mother at
Warningcamp in Sussex,
Summer 1940*

2.
*Held by my grandfather
Dr. Ernest Peake,
who delivered me, 1940*

3.
With my father
at Warningcamp, 1940

4.
A portrait
at the age of one,
January 1941

5.
Wearing my father's
army cap,
Summer 1941

6.
*With my father, outside the cottage
at 94, Wepham, March 1942*

7.
The Peake family boating on the River Arun,
in 1944 – the episode when I nearly drowned took place very
soon after this photograph was taken

8.
*My brother
Fabian in
Picture Post
1945*

9.
*On Sark with
Armand the gardener*

10.
*On Sark with
Judy the donkey*

11.
My father on Sark, 1946

12.
*My brother and I on Sark, dressed for the visit
of Princess Elizabeth*

13.
*With Fabian, dressed as clowns for the
Sark Carnival, July 1948*

was closing down, and he and I would often find yet more bones on walks – bones of rabbits or other dead animals. We would make them into invented skeletons, then half bury them in out of the way places and tell my mother that we had found a body. She wouldn't always come and see, so I would have to pretend to be going for a walk, thereby accidentally coming across the dead body my father and I had planted earlier. Half covered with leaves, it looked very authentic indeed, and we would invent some famous murder or violent happening that had occurred, and deem ourselves the discoverers. I don't know if she believed us, but as the skull was real and the tibias and fibulas from the same museum, the cattle, sheep and rabbit bones suitably ordered, all looked authentic enough. But the most lovely of all were the large collection of those whale bones, which at first numbered twenty or so and which were sometimes arranged in a snaking line, progressively getting smaller as they wound across the sitting room, starting at the fireplace. During the many moves, most somehow disappeared.

Once, on finding a dead rat in a lane, my father drew it, seeing a dignity in the rodent. Here was its unpleasant grey colour, its awful tail immobile, stretching out so far from its flanks, but this rat which now hangs on a wall in my house has grace, for my father caught the life in its death, the helpless paws caught in an innocent supplicatory gesture, as though they were gripping something. His drawing even brought out the rat's own individuality in its position on the path. I wonder if its being dead made it more attractive to him. Rats were endemic in Belsen: perhaps this later drawing somehow showed the rat as the dying Jews he had seen there.

On wild days on Sark my brother, my father and I, dressed in sou'westers, wellington boots and macs, would all leave the house, and walk up past the windmill - a defunct and small Sancho Panza magnet - along the stony roads to Grand Greve. This bay, against which on wild days the sea would rage, was a wonderful sight when viewed from 300 feet up. The isthmus linking Big and Little Sark, called

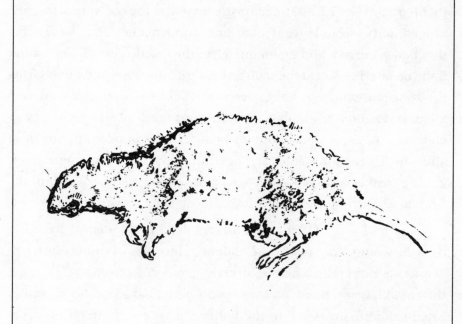

Dead rat, Burpham

Sebastian, Circa 1951

La Coupee, had on one side this usually sheltered beach, and on the other – 300 feet below – the amethyst and topaz beach. On the wildest of days, if my father wasn't working, we would descend the zig-zag path downwards, through the bushes at the top, treading carefully on the muddy steps, for rain on these chosen days of wildness often accompanied the discomfort. Nearer the bottom of the cliff, the only concession to the modern life were about twenty poorly constructed concrete steps, the final one was about two feet above the shingle, from which we both would make a yell as our feet struck the stones and sand of the beach. We would head off to the left of the beach, for here we could see the violent meeting of the five currents at their most powerful. Great sea horses and spray ten, fifteen feet high, would dance in a foaming clash aiming into the dark sky. Ever changing the shape was for a split second recorded in the eye, but then would evaporate almost immediately, to be replaced by another permutation. We would perch on hard granite rocks, as near to the seas as possible, almost on the edge of drowning, as the sea rose higher, and the chasm closed between the rock we were sitting on and the beach, until a great leap through the foam found us on terra firma again. All over the island, from the northern point at L'Eperquerie, with the rocks tapering little by little into the sea, to the southern tip by the tin mines by Venus Pool, the seas pounded Sark like no other place I have known. Every time my father took me out, from the primordial days of January when storms would lash the tiny island, to summer days, as when I was eight and my father, Louis MacNiece and others explored the caves and cliffs, rocks and caverns, with a background of the softest of lappings of tiny voices – the meterological perfection of 'calm'; on all occasions the darkness of the banked depths around Sark always suggested power to us. A power which is caught both in *Moby Dick* and in the gripping poem my father wrote about the terrible retribution wrought on the mutineers, *The Touch o'The Ash*.

As a child, I was always an adequate swimmer, but

a show off too. I would wait for an audience, then run like mad down to the sea and stay underwater, counting up until I felt the entire world would be waiting with bated breath for me to surface. I could often quite frighten myself, however, especially in fairly high seas, when I would go out so far that I lost sight of where I had started from. This was all in the cause of being noticed, but on laboriously swimming back, a task sometimes made harder by an outgoing and strong tide, it would prove to have been virtually useless, as no-one had even noticed my efforts. This and many other similar childish endeavours I think I must, in part, have inherited. Even in later life, my mother would dance wonderfully on our famous table to flamenco music at the end of her parties, as she always liked to encourage other people to dance. She would attend parties with magnificent great feather boas around her neck and click castanets she had been given in Spain. The guests would clap and cheer her and she would yell back, "Olé!".

In his earliest days on Sark my father would take enormous risks that were commented on far and wide. He would climb sheer rock faces and suspend himself above caverns and once, caught by a large octopus while exploring a cave, emerged with its tendrils securely locked around his right leg. After prising the creature off him by clubbing and knifing it, my father displayed the hundreds of suction marks as signs of virility and daring. Riding on his bicycle, standing on the saddle or the handle bars, one foot on each, was another of his tricks, a hazardous one, as I found to my cost on trying to emulate it. He too was a good swimmer and we would swim together in Dixcart Bay and try to clap hands underwater, to no audible avail.

From my bedroom I could see the French coast on clear days, but I could also see the ferry the 'Sarnia', quite clearly sometimes, although it was often several miles out. From my bedroom, from the warmth, security and inviolability of my home, what seemed the terrible heavings, plungings, even the final movements of the ship in violent storms, made me feel for the poor passengers, who would later include me. From my vantage point I would have a feeling, so common in children, when the tingling sensation of knowing that one's own safety is in a way at the expense of others gives one the most glorious of temptations towards unwitting smugness. There but for the grace of God, and on the stormy sea people are being terribly ill, they're afraid, they long for journey's end, but I am safe, I am secure and there they are, stiff upper lip perhaps, as the 'Sarnia' went out of sight past the North East of the island. It was a false security though, because I knew that I lived on an island, that there were no aeroplanes, no bridges to the mainland, no firm stones across the deep, dark water. I knew that one day I would have to cross it, and that it would be rough. I was right - the day I had to go to Guernsey for the first time was very stormy. Later in 1949, in my last term at Les Vauxblets, I crossed from Weymouth to St Peter Port in a severe storm, a force eleven gale, and the journey took two days instead of six hours. I had had a bunk reserved in a cabin with another person and it was in the bowels of the ship. Giants of the deep hammered against the porthole from which nothing could be seen in the darkness of Weymouth. As it left the harbour, before even reaching the open water, the ship had lurched over at such an angle that all the crockery was thrown across the small restaurant and smashed. "The journey," said the Captain, "will take somewhat longer than is normal and our expected arrival time cannot be given. All seats on the ship have been secured where possible; it is advised to hold the sides of your bunk, if you have one, for stability." The storm of that January night, and the parting at Waterloo Station from my parents, which seemed like a century before, will never leave me. We had to stay outside St Peter Port for eight hours because we could not dock. When the 'Sarnia' was finally tied up, I cried with relief.

My mother captured, in many oil paintings, the storm bedraggled lanes and byways of the island; after particularly bad ones, she would take out pencil and paper and draw or paint the trees wildly lurching away from the winds. Storms during my time on

Sark seemed ubiquitous, exciting and dramatic, but were most comfortably observed from behind my curtain on the first floor of my home. My father and my mother always saw things in terms of their artistic content. An old man's face, a giraffe or antelope, a ballet dancer or frog, a map of Kent or a shape like France - anything had in it the potential to arouse the artist. If you look at clouds, you can see a thousand shapes, my parents would tell me. And they're there. Who could guess what that shape reminded one of? Often, when looking into the sky, my father would try to guess the shape that my mother had seen in it, and my brother or I would try as well. Just as one can tap out, on a desk or on a table, a favourite song and ask for the tune to be guessed at, so it was with the clouds: "Just like Mrs Somebody's hat, just like the butcher's nose or the parish priest's head", we would reply.

The main island of Sark held in its tiny grasp the Robert Louis Stevenson power of the gorse heathland and the high adventure of summer's idyll. On some days, sandwiches rolled up in our towels, our swimming costumes on under the short grey trousers we wore, my brother and I would set off for the 'Hole in the rock' above one of the beaches and throw stones the 50 feet down onto the empty stony strand below, while seagulls, the buzzing of flies and the heady smell of gorse and fern surrounded us, before the steep and precipitous climb down. Once, carried away by strong winds Fabian was swept out by the powerful current and, like myself at an earlier stage, was rescued. He, like me, had lost consciousness, and the presence of a medical friend who was with us on this whole family day out, saved him. These outings were mostly with my parents' friends. The poet Louis MacNeice and his wife stayed once and took us on walks. He later sent a short poem about his stay and dedicated it to the 'blue eyed thugs', as he christened my brother and myself.

• • •

I am afraid the countryside in its technical specific sense, as a place made up of species identified with scientific detachment, did not figure in our lives – and as far as I can remember I never was taught to differentiate between types of tree, bird, crop or mineral. My father could quote from books verbatim, could recite complete poems if given only the first line from the works of Shelley or Wordsworth, De la Mare or Byron, but wouldn't know the latin name of a species of common tree. On the other hand, he could, just by my showing a square inch of paint from one of my parent's large collection of art books, tell me the painter. I would place a piece of paper right across a reproduction of a Picasso or a Monet, a Chagal or a Constable, even old masters - the tip of a finger from a Van Dyck or Vermeer - all were known to him by the minutest of details. Trees as clinically defined plants did not figure very highly up the agenda of priorities. But trees in the sense of shape, like clouds: that was another thing. My father's inexhaustible imagination could make a burnt-out tree stump in Kent, or the ancient oaks in a wood near Salisbury, into things with the most eerie and frightening primaeval malevolence about them, could make them into living, dancing creatures in a thousand descriptions of their beauty, ugliness, majesty and sheer powerfulness, giving them an instant life. Trees blown down by storms affected him the same way. The centuries of gales made sure that a walk along La Segneurie road from the cross-roads on the middle of the island, to the northern tip, took one past gnarled, broken, weather-beaten and ancient trees, which gave him shapes of huddling men and women trying to keep out the inevitable fate of eventual, ageing death.

Each summer the annual fete was held, when all the islanders were invited to the main field in the centre of the island. They had fancy dress parades, egg and spoon races, the sack race, running races, tombolas and prizes. My father had made a tray with

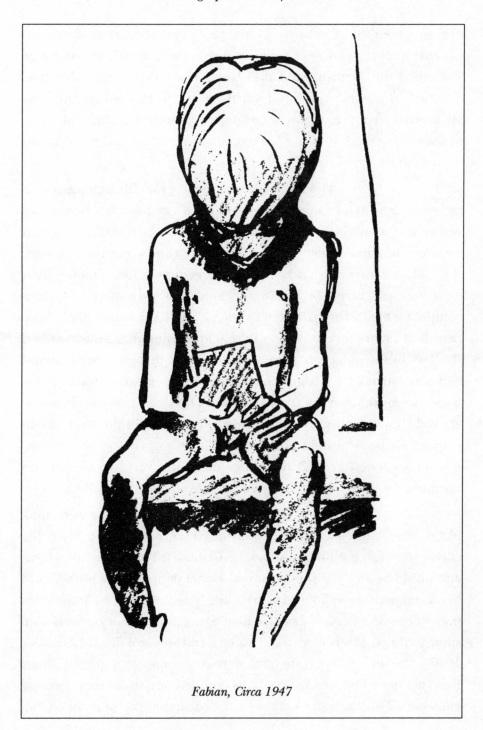

Fabian, Circa 1947

a glass glued to it, which I held aloft and would suddenly tip towards people, who were convinced that the glass filled with water would fall off, bruising and drenching them. As it was, the glass attached to the tray just spilt a little water, but stayed on the tray. My brother wore a clown's costume, painted cheeks and eyes, with a top hat and stick he looked like one of the Bertram Mills's professionals.

The main event of the day for children was a slow bicycle race which I entered one year. The reward was a hamper of sweets, and as sweets were rationed, these Aero bars, Mars bars, and assorted chocolates were far more of a luxury and rarity than they are now. The starting pistol rang out and forgetting or being mesmerised by winning, I tore off at a mad speed, easily beating the other competitors with their strange slowness. Why the 'slow' part of the race didn't make an impression I don't know, but once I was declared the 'last' by the judge and the peals of laughter that greeted my arrival had really struck me, I found that even my parents' explanations were quite incomprehensible. I arrived first so I had won; now it seemed you arrived first so you were **last**. These ideas taxed brain power to an extent that both hunted and haunted. 'You're first so you're last' remained etched graphically, poignantly, and very emotionally on my mind for years, as the humiliation was so painfully public.

On Wednesdays the great event of the week took place in the hall. Next to the churchyard this green painted and faded corrugated iron building was also the Island Parliament or Chief Pleas and would be also the venue for occasional dances. The horsedrawn black ambulance was housed nearby, and here the St John's Ambulance man would occasionally practice bandaging arms and legs. This high spot was the weekly film with the trailers, cartoon or B films. In the late 1940's, the secondary crime films were sometimes so poor, with their ham actors and transparent plots and chases, that they became comedies. The laughter from the hall was deafening as the actor on film was saying deathless lines: 'take that you cur' or 'I'll get you for that Smith', as everyone reacted in feigned shock, guffawing and squealing whinneys of sarcastic mirth.

When the lights went off and the turning of the reel for the big film audibly announced its imminence, a hush would come over the sixpenny section for, as Alan de Cartaret, a local friend of mine, would always say to any main film at all to be shown there, it was 'supposed to be good' in a broad Sarkese dialect. My favourites were the Will Hay films which made me cry with laughter, but the old ukelele player George Formby, Charlie Chaplin and the early Tarzan of Johnny Weismuller held us all in their grip. It was the pure Hollywood enchantment of Deanna Durbin that really bowled me over. Captivated, head over heels in unrequited love, transported to heaven on the backs of soaring, melifluous but sentimental violins, she captured the whole of me. Dreaming of her, dazzled by her naive and openly sweet nature, I saw no sugary transience here, just the pull of the first woman I fell in love with.

To get to the hall from our house we could leave through a hedge at the back of the garden, across the side of the large field next to it and through the graveyard by the church. On summer evenings when the light was still up, this part of the walk was easy. In winter, howling gales would often cross the island and add to the sound of the branches creaking and cracking in the trees. The blowing gusts of January nights through the graveyard were bad enough on the way **to** the film. **After** a Lon Chaney thriller, an Edgar Allan Poe adaptation or a Dickens masterpiece, the return across the graveyard was that particular horror come true. As there were no lights on Sark, it was straight out of the hall and a few muttered goodbyes, see you next week, or tomorrow or whatever, then the walk became a 'Whistling in the Dark' mad dash. Sometimes I had to take a younger boy or girl back over to Little Sark. After dropping them off I was on my own, I would race like one possessed on the return journey up the other side of the

Coupee, racing along the straight road, with only the wild whistling of the telegraph wires above for company. I would get to the crossroads, and still flat out, pass the doctor's house on one side and the two teachers' bungalow on the other. Our gate, a wide cross bar style, was set back 15 feet from the lane and pulling back the black metal securing arm, I rushed up the gravel drive and into the house. All the way back, voices I thought I heard would say "I'm just behind you" or "Not long now until I catch you." Tingling, my blood streaming through my veins, I felt the spirit of boyhood eager for adventure: "Jim Hawkins, a hero from *Treasure Island*, wouldn't have quaked", I used to say to myself, "stop breathing for a second", which I would then do, and pain would course through the young body, living at its highest pitch of excitement.

We had a donkey which came with the house, called Judy. She was grey and quite large. I loved her, but I thought she could do more than just stand around, either in the house, which caused great amusement to visitors, or outside the front window: I felt she could be put to more enterprising purposes. The man from whom we leased the house had some traps and even though I was not yet eight, I put my idea to him, that I harness the animal to one of these, and take trippers on rides round the island. There was a group of carriages always ready for hire at the top of the harbour hill. It was an idea that worked, for at the end of the first day I'd given five rides at sixpence each, and half a crown in 1947 was quite a bit of money.

We hadn't long been on Sark when I started nagging my parents to take me to Herm, and finally I did go on a day trip to see Shell Beach, the famous sheltered bay that collects all the drifting molluscs ebbing their way south eastwards, carried by the Gulf Stream. In the event my parents didn't take me; I was taken by some Sarkese friends. We went on a 20 foot long wooden boat, completely open, with cross benches and a rear seat for the passengers and powered by a small mid-engine.

Donkey, Sark, 1949

The day had started off slightly breezy and although there was a slight swell on the sea over from Sark, the wind became quite strong as we left on the return journey in our little open boat. About half way back, the grey clouds became thunderous and the first drops of rain fell on us. We did not have long to wait before the full wrath of heaven was unleashed and the seas began to swell. Although only a few miles, the journey took two hours and towards the end I began to panic, so I stood up on top of the engine housing, which was in the middle of the boat, and in a voice of real fear began to shout "Jesus save us, Jesus save us". In sight of Sark the engine started to splutter and one of the most terrifying hours of my life ended eventually as the little boat limped into Creux by the skill of the pilot. I have been haunted by the apparently tiny gulf between the boat reaching harbour and capsizing ever since.

Our style of living on Sark was relaxed but unnerved others unused to it. Judy the donkey walked about the house shocking the midwife brought in for the birth of my sister Clare. When Leon Goosens, who played his oboe in our sitting room, came to stay, Judy, who had found the front door open, passed the open sitting room door and walked upstairs into the bedroom, where my mother was nursing a three day old daughter. The temporary nurse, Mrs Kilfoyle, who my father christened Tinfoil, found this too much, packed her bags and was gone by the same evening. This wasn't the first time the animal had made an appearance, as two days before the birth while her back was turned to the open door as she was discussing arrangements with the local doctor, Judy had ambled in and bitten her ear. She shrieked, which probably didn't do my mother in labour upstairs much good.

Armand the Moroccan gardener loved to rake the gravel path until symmetrical lines stretched from the gate to the larger area in front of the house. The donkey would tramp about and undo the painstaking work and Armand would rake it again. Once on a walk

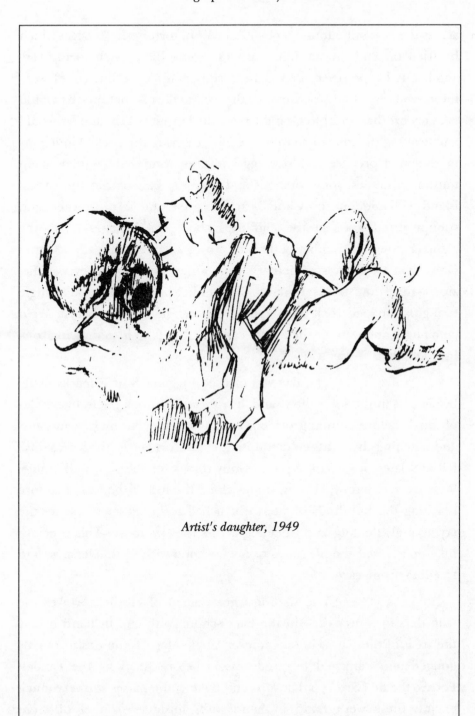

Artist's daughter, 1949

across the island, he found a beautiful pair of tortoiseshell glasses which he tried on and saw nothing through them, his eyesight being very good, but he persevered until he'd ruined his eyes, but could wear these symbols, as he saw them, of the well-to-do. Sometimes he would take my brother and I to Grand Greve, the largest beach, and we would amble along the mile or so with one of us carrying the packed lunch my mother had prepared. Moist egg and cress sandwiches under damp muslin, tomatoes, some oranges and maybe a banana, on the carless island with hidden coves and beaches, gorse and fern, bracken and stumpy dried grass at the cliff tops above the beaches made the clamber down the simple paths adventures all those days ago. Grand Greve had 645 very rudimentary steps which we counted every time, zig-zagging downwards towards the sand. At low tide a tall single triangular shaped rock was exposed on one side of the beach. We'd climb up it and wait for the tide to come in, hopping in and racing back inshore when it was a few feet deep.

The day was marked by giant S or F marks made by big toes in the soft yellow sand, by races to the rock pools, by nibbles of lunch before climbing the big rock again, by counting cormorants and watching the lights come on in St Peter Port across the sea as dusk fell and later by packing up our sandy things for the slow walk home. We were very happy, kicking stones along the top of the beach, before reaching the hundreds of steps which had to be climbed, eyeing the crying gulls floating and wheeling across the sky above. This precious time epitomised the pleasures of my boyhood with its timelessness and freedom from care.

The sizzling wheaty smell of Horlicks evokes the cold days of winter time in the Sark school, with cup in hand before the treat of the day: schools radio or Uncle Mac. Little desks roughly gouged and damaged by predecessors before the war: the Guilles, Perres, the de Carterets, Lanyons and Bakers; the patois still very much extant, these went hand in hand with outsiders from a different

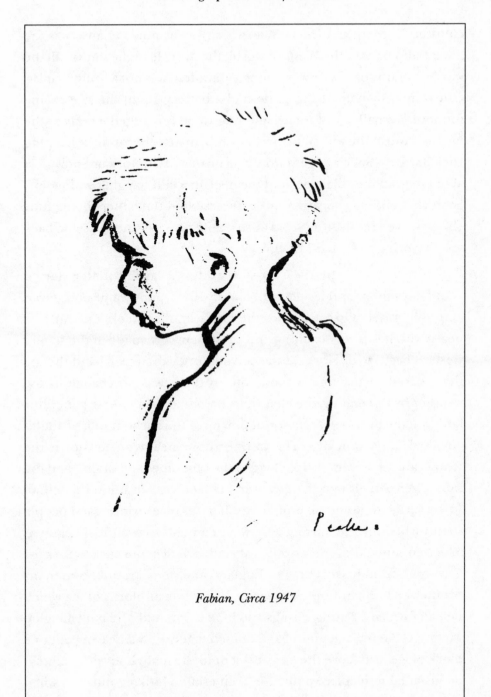

Fabian, Circa 1947

culture. Listening to Uncle Mac, which seems now so naive, was the great radio treat of the Western world, the miracle of the sound 'all the way from London' as we were often reminded, was not a thing to miss. Our own aptly-named Pye radio had a battery about the size of one found in a small car of today, and had to be recharged weekly at the bicycle shop at the top of the harbour hill, or else the far more exciting Dick Barton – Special Agent would be missed. With Jock or Snowy just about to grab the villain around the neck in a cliff-hanging ending in a Scottish glen, the evocative music necessitated the battery being fully charged even if for three years or so a mile one way and the same back was the price to be paid in energy.

In 1947 a really wild and lasting winter started about November and lasted until March 1948. Snow came and stayed and obliterated a great deal of the landscape for weeks on end. To begin with it was very exciting and snowmen were made in the school yard; to begin with Horlicks was served hotter than usual and the log fires roared in the tiny school. But as there was no change in the weather by December, the electricity was cut off due to the generator failing at the little power station at the top of the harbour hill, attitudes changed fairly quickly. The lasting snow meant no let up in the temperatures' low level. Ice clogged the rain pipes and drains, and the rain water barrels were frozen over. The power was off in the school so we were sent home early on in this famous bleak winter; and people soon wished for the Spring, a thaw and an end to what had begun as a heaven-sent childrens' novelty. My father had come back to Sark for Christmas from his teaching in England and one day, unknown to my brother or I, he got up very early. Using lots of blocks of ice which he had formed by using casings and boxes as moulds, he built an igloo with carved entrance tunnel and domed main room. Leaving out one block of ice just above the end adjacent to the main body of the thing, he installed in its place a picture of an eskimo looking out, and when we were called to come and see his handiwork there was this grinning eskimo to greet us. With our cherished gauntlets on, wellington boots, scarves wrapping us up, we tore out of the house, down the tunnel and into the little house where some blankets had been laid across the ground over the earth he had cleared of snow.

It took a long time for the ice and snow to melt that winter and that last little pile of ice which marked the final end of the igloo stays as a poignant memory of all that I so longed for and loved about what it was to have a father who could do that for us. "This is where my igloo was," I would say to people when they would come to stay, or to friends or locals who came to the house. "It lasted weeks and weeks," I'd say. "My dad made it."

Archery, an ancient and dignified art, had taken a hold of my father about the summer of 1948, and he brought back from London a whole set of bows, arrows and lovely canvas-covered targets in bright colours of red for the bull's eye, blue and white for other scores. This canvas held a tightly packed straw body to the board and in summer my parents used the garden for archery practice. They had long slender quivers and bows of different shapes and sizes in yew and ash. They loved the singing sound of the arrow, the silence just before and after the shot, the simplicity of the act of firing

Once to see, I suppose, what would happen, my father fired directly above him with the largest yew bow, pulling the gut to full force and letting fly the arrow, which sailed into the sunlight to descend at a murderous pace a foot or two away from my brother standing nearby.

At the time, and, I wonder, did I ever behave differently, I needed so much attention that people would sometimes in later life despair of me. As a boy an *idee fixe* would seize me: I remember wanting a dog, I would not give up, for weeks, the chant of "I want a dog", "I want a dog", which would echo around the house in Sark until, just accidentally like an arrow that had landed on my head, the chant might stop. My father's method of silencing me at this time remains engrained; and that was to put my head just between his knees and hold me there for a long, long time. Snuffed out, my current demand would be forgotten in my relief on being released, only to start again when I judged the atmosphere right. I must have been an awful experience for my parents, for the 'hairbrush' on the hand or backside I received from my mother when my father was back in London was a frequent punishment. I would go up to my parents' bedroom and really get whacked, but I loved my mother very much, and I think her knowledge of this love meant that she couldn't produce the cold, dispassionate presence needed to mete out physical punishment in its most effective form.

When I was about nine my father gave me an unbirthday present: a bow of my own. He already had his bow and my mother had hers. We would stand some way from the target and try to hit the bull's eye. The grass grew quite long at the sides of the very large garden on Sark and in that very hot summer, when flies and insects, birds and the quacking of our ducks on the little man-made pond in the garden, all expostulated their freedom of movement and life, the arrows sailed with various intensities of sound in the direction of the target. I loved that bow, but the only difficulty was that after particularly athletic strainings to create maximum velocity, the gut would snap out from its nick at the top of the bow and limply hang down and the bow would regain the semi-straight shape. My father would then deftly place the bow against his left knee, press forward and re-attach the string. Whenever I tried, the bow would shoot off at an angle, because my knee was nowhere near the grip at half way mark, so it spun awry. One day I was so angry with not being able to restring my present that I threw away the bow as far as I could and it landed in undergrowth. I ran around the garden screaming that this bow was stupid and "I'm glad it's lost". I didn't know if it was or not, for my parents, probably having had enough of me and archery for the day had gone off somewhere else. Later, after leaving, I'm sure, a small trail of destruction all over the place, I went to look for the bow. I hunted and hunted, but as I was in such a temper when I threw it away, now I couldn't find my unbirthday present. I shouted and screamed for assistance; none was forthcoming. I screamed again and again. Other people were doing their own things. My brother with his tribe of Sioux attacking the cavalry behind the windmill or catching fish in the translucent waters of the old Creux harbour built in Napoleon's time. At any rate I had to find it myself, but I didn't. My noise continued. There must have been a point when another string broke, that of the nerve leading to my parents' patience with me. My father took hold of me, put my head between his legs, and despite entreaties, cries of help and supplication, there I remained. Whether the claustrophobia from which I suffer still began on that high summer day I don't know, but I can imagine my head placed in the same position and feel again the blackness of physical control, and my inability to do a thing about it. I was released, but not before I was blue in the face, frightened and humiliated. Quite right too, for I had caused the day to shatter. I found my bow eventually, but never fired it with the same keenness again.

My father knew many people destined for the top of their own tree. A constant friend was Dr. Gordon Smith, an academic with a unique command of Chinese culture and history and a great advocate of my father's many talents. He was a great support in the early days: days of *The Moccus*, a collaborative book project worked on for many years but never published. During the years when *Titus* was being written he was a good critic and friend, supportive and helpful. In later years this influence waned and they geographically and in spirit drifted apart. During my early life in Sark, he would come over to stay and he would take either myself or my brother and I for dare-devil walks and show the exact spots where he and my father nearly came to grief a decade earlier. He was the most marvellous story teller and wove magnificently intricate stories, so that at the end, spellbound, we could have been in the Congo, the Nile

Road to Little Sark, 1948

Clare, Sark, 1949

Delta, or the Gobi, for all my brother or I knew. He had an educated soft voice with inflections that held one gripped at salient points, but it was in the telling of ghost stories that he showed his full talent. We had no electricity for the first two years in Sark, and at night, when the wind howled, he would keep a particularly gruesome and cold story for the time the light had gone, then when huddled around the Aladdin oil stove, he would begin his story. The hair on our heads standing on end, he would sometimes cut off the story in mid-stream and ask, "Who's that?" about a noise the wind had made. This petrified us even more, then he would continue, reaching the denoument slowly, deliberately, culminating sometimes in an unexpected wild shriek. We would be practically beside ourselves with frozen fear at this point, at which he would say, "Time for bed now, boys," as though asking if we would like another cup of tea. Even into our late teenage years, when he used to stay in our Wallington house, he would tell stories, sometimes even not flinching from addressing lots of our friends - up to ten or twelve sometimes. Gordon Smith, or Goatie as he was always known - a nickname my father had given him - drifted out of our lives after Wallington. That was really when my father began the beginnings of his illnesses: he could not cope, I think, with watching the disintegration of his best and only real friend.

Of all my father's paintings my favourite shows me the day of the rentree, and a sadness permeates the picture: the hopeless, helpless look of the boy not ripe for ejection from the bosom of the family, from a peace that I must have so tried to disrupt. This painting, haunting as it is and depicting a dark mood of solitary incomprehension, poses questions when I look at it now, perfectly observed and executed

In Kenneth Grahame's masterpiece *The Wind in the Willows*, the apogee of homesickness, the hatred of the forced separation brought about for whatever reason so poignantly shows the human condition through animal shadows. Mole's rediscovery of his home and his nest and his own place in the world is powerfully put as 'Moley smelt his little hole again': This is the coming home I talk of, and always remember.

With my trunk packed at the door, the wait for the carriage going to the harbour, Armand at hand to say farewell, the cat Chlöe haring up and down the palm tree, the Khaki Campbell ducks quacking on the little pond and the look on my mother's face was always too much for me. My brother's phlegmatic "Oh blow" when the moment of farewell came, was so much braver, philosophical and strong, I caved in to something too big to be contemplated. Down the hill, the creaking wheels over the gravel lanes, along the avenue with its corrugated iron shops to the Carrafour and the descent past the running streams on either side of the harbour hill and the sea. This journey towards another world was like a last journey. On days of rough seas my fear became palpable. I could hardly get on the boat for fear of the unknown, I would grip the handles when on board and ask Jesus to save me, to bring me to some sort of equanimity, to be in control, to try to be calm enough to stand alone, but not frightened or afraid. No one was ever any real help, I tried to be brave, to pretend I wasn't in a type of pain which I still feel acutely, but somehow it never worked.

The wonderful days of boyhood and the lack of responsibility gave the illusion, real at this age of innocence, that nothing was answerable for or to. Heady days in the beating winds that crowd the rocky lanes and hedgerows of Sark. How I loved the wind, watching the 'sea horses' as my father called them, that others were sailing on. Often they were calm, but it seemed the balance was in favour of the rough ride. I hated every minute of being away from home, I was only seven years old when I first went away to boarding school, and each parting was like being pulled off a rock, as though the limpet I felt I was should not be prised off. However I was, for the first time, and my packing done, my trunk painted by my father with my name beautifully painted on the outside with counterpoint colour, nearly filled with the necessary pairs of everything arranged inside, I waited in the hall downstairs. I cried with tears that dazzled me. I always hoped for a reprieve, though this ploy never worked.

Down the harbour hill I went with both my parents, if my father was not away teaching in London. The tiny distance from the house to the boat taking me away, not more than three quarters of a mile was like the walk to the gallows. And on the boat, at either Creux harbour if the sea was calm, or La Maseline if rough, the wrench I always dreaded even into late youth took place. When the ropes splashed down into the water, and there came the slow reversing out from the jetty to the open waters where the boat could turn round for it to head off, it was that tug which the hangman gives the feet to make sure the neck is broken that I felt.

No alleviation to my misery was found in being in new surroundings, in places to discover or in new boys to meet. At this time the nooks and crannies of home, the toys, dens, hiding places, the rope ladders up the trees, the dank, watery smell of the bunker the German occupation force had built in the garden of the chalet, these were everything to me.

But I had to go, and I went to school in Guernsey to a college run by Christian brothers, the first half of their title often at odds with their behaviour. Some were sadists, others latent homosexuals or other oddities who didn't do a great deal for my general education in any subject as far as I can remember. Becoming champion at two highly intellectual subjects, weight lifting and roller skating, was about the apex of my achievements.

On being sent away to boarding school at the age of eight, I felt bereft. I quote the short letter below, that I sent before we were granted permission to write home, which was only given after a month into the new term. Pocket money was not allowed, and stamps

Sebastian, Circa 1948

could only be bought from the headmaster, so having stolen the paper and envelope, I finally stole the stamp by going through his study to find one. Then, in September 1948, I wrote to my parents for the first time:

> *Sebastian*
> *... Dear Mummy I do do wish you would come O please come mummy come mummy   Seddy*

This letter, from Les Vauxblets College, Guernsey, was followed by others, not always quite so pleading for a return home, but all similar in tone. Once, following the discovery of the arms dump, (of which more later), I did write very excitedly in a happier frame of mind:

> *Les Vauxblets*
> *...dear mummy and fay i hope you are well i am bringing some*
> *nives and too helmets one for fay and one for me i got them*
> *from the gurmen tunels in the tunels it was very smely and a*
> *boy went with a candle and set the tunels on fire with love*
> *from Sebb*

Gloom descended again, and long before the next half term arrived, I was feeling very lonely and disturbed, living incarcerated in what felt like, and resembles, an impenetrable, dark castle. The pleading continued:

> *dear mummy i am looking forward to seeing you dear mummy i want*
> *you to come over and get me at half term i am sending these nots*

and they are called testimon, tales and will you sine them at the

back and send back as soon as you can with lots of love from sebby

Finally, the Christmas holiday was approaching and in my fourth Vauxblets letter to my mother and fay, - Fabian my younger brother - I wrote:

...dear mummy and fay i hope you are well we went to the end of

the island and had a nice time i climbed a big rock there. i am

lokiking forward to Christmas with love from Sebastian

I inherited all my mother's correspondence, letters and writings after she died and amongst them all I found every letter I had ever written her, which she had kept chronologically and had marked them, '1st letter', '2nd letter' and so on. They must have been quite precious to her. For the son of not one but two writers, my handwriting was awful, for I was already eight when the first one was written. Ungrammatical, rather tragic and naive, I used only lower case, misspelt my own nickname, and signed myself in each of the four quoted with a different name. I always felt myself to be very unhappy as a boy, and that perhaps submerged somewhere in my being, there was something stunting my ability to listen and learn. Then, only one year later and just before the last half term before being sent to my next boarding school, I wrote in quite clear writing and in ink - all the previous letters had been in pencil -

Dear mummy and daddy. I hope you are. I am very well thank you

for the parcels you sent me there is only 1 week and 6 days till

half term and then you sead that daddy would send me one of

thoes modeled aeroplanes to play with in the roady room. thre
lites went out on tuesday and Brother Charles told us a gost
story of when he was going on his bike when he sor sparks
comming out of the grave and a figure of a gost coming out of
the gra

pto.

ve

   With love from
   Sebby and fai

(My brother joined me at Les Vauxblets for a couple of terms in the winter of 1949). At the end of the letter I executed a strange drawing before signing myself again underneath.

The drawing is of a ghost-like apparition emerging from a coffin, his arms and legs shackled in awful looking metal clamps which pinion him. From a bubble he is saying 'i am a gost'. The letter ends:

...'from sebby', under that drawing. The words 'from sebby' are incorporated into the body of the coffin, and it is probably this fixation with death and its doings that gave rise to the ubiquitous doodlings of coffins and coffin shaped boxes with the crucifix always embossed on top during the unhappy years of my failed marriage.

I used to be teased about my Christian name and was bullied quite a bit, but I learned early on that surreptitiousness helped to keep me from the major bullies' attention. I picked up the facility of appearing so innocent that even if I were the culprit of an escapade I didn't get the blame.

There was a Spaniard there who used to pick frogs up by their hind legs and with a machete type knife slice them in two to watch the legs continue to squirm after dissection. Later he became more adventurous and created a primitive type of pistol which I used to watch him making. One night he went out of the dormitory and shot a cow to see what would happen; It died later and he was expelled.

Fights in the dormitory between enemies were arranged for after lights out at 7 p.m. and were quite vicious. When I couldn't get out of one, as I'd been seen as the culprit in someone's eyes, then I would do my best, but these nocturnal events rarely involved me. I was much busier listening to someone or other's crystal set under the sparse bedclothes.

This order of Catholic educationalists believed in strict regimes for young boys: the windows were left open at night, only one blanket was allowed and a 6 a.m. rise was the order of things. In the mornings the brother on duty would come into the dormitory clapping his hands loudly (still echoing in my ears to this day) and if one didn't get up immediately, then, on his return journey down the line of the double tiered bunks, he would pull all the bedclothes off and beat the offender. As the windows were left open, even in winter, it was often freezing and immediately on getting up out of bed, we had to form two queues fanning out from the first in line just outside the wash basins. Strict silence was maintained and any noise resulted in 'the shower'. That was the punishment meted out for any minor infraction. It could have been seen as a special privilege to have a shower cubicle to oneself, if it hadn't been for the fact that icy cold water was used, and some of these brothers in Christ would deliberately take the soap from the dish in the cubicle, drop it on the base of the shower, then demand its being picked up, and with the culprit's back to him, would then rain blows on the boy's backside.

Dressed, we marched in lines down to Mass, which we had every day just to remind us, I suppose, of forgiveness, humility and love, before the silence of breakfast in the refectory. Talking was only allowed occasionally, when the high table and the headmaster and his lackeys ordained. No free-for-all ever ensued, but subdued mutterings, as fear of far worse treatment than the soap dropping (or the 'chocolate' that I had yet to experience), would be the consequences of the pent up enthusiasm of wild boys from six to fifteen years of age. I don't expect any of the parents of the 180 or so boys during the 1940's at this College would have believed stories of the cruelty and ignorance that went on at this supposed place of education.

I had only been at the place some three weeks when, as a result of not answering a question correctly, I was brought before the class and asked if I would like some chocolate. "Yes Sir", was my fairly greedy reply, at which the chuckling from some of the class should have warned me that chocolate was the one thing I wouldn't be getting. "Hand out, boy", the master said, "Would you like a big piece or a little?" "A small piece, sir," I said, hoping to have caught on a bit to the clue in a sense I'd been given by some of the class. With that the stick he had been holding behind his back came down with a memorable swish on my outstretched hand. This happened not once but six times, with blood drawn from the soft area at the base of the right thumb testifying to its being a 'chocolate' worth having. Boys answering "a big piece" got six on each hand. The boys' pact of silence concerning the punishment I broke on behalf of the new boys of the following year, a disclosure for which I paid dearly, not only from the old timers but from this same sadistic brother. He chose me to grasp Jesus's suffering at Easter by being given holly leaves to wear, next to my skin under my shirt, which he ground into my chest with vigour.

The atmosphere of the place was strangely one of aimlessness. Although classes started on time, and routine marked the day to lights out, the war, (which had only just finished) the occupation of Guernsey throughout the duration; and the fact that tanks and guns left by the Germans were still on the playing fields nine months after liberation, all made for a frustrated feeling of directionless change.

The great drama of the place was supplied by Brother Charles. He was tall, well built, quite handsome and a poor

14.
The Peake family at Le Grand Greve, Sark, 1947

15.
The family with
Louis Macneice
and his wife,
Sark 1948

16.
Taken by my mother on Sark

17.
*With my mother, as I was about to leave
for my catholic boarding school*

18.
Family group, Sark

19.
Le Chalet, Sark – before

20.
Le Chalet, Sark – after

21.
Clare and my father at Smarden, 1951

22.
Smarden

23.
Smarden

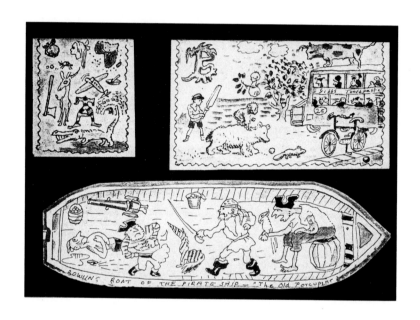

24.
*Drawings from the autograph book
that my father gave me*

teacher. What he loved most was to take his chosen pupils with him on his trips around the island at night and, leaving after lights out, he would drive them out on secret missions in the Fordson lorry that belonged to the College, and which was usually used for taking the farm produce from the school to St Peter Port on market days. This open backed, three ton lorry had a flat metal floor and 13 inch wooden side boards, and seemed to always be in very good condition. I think it was his pride and joy.

I was still, at about eight and a half years old, a bit too young to have gained favour with him as an older 'chosen one' would do, but as the academic side of things didn't so much impress him and it had come to his attention that I consistently came top at roller skating and weight lifting, I think he must have felt that I had the makings of one of his nocturnal accomplices.

Nothing was ever spoken about what they all did at night, but little by little, finding my way into the inner sanctum of the special group, it came to light that these trips had something to do with taking notes on smuggling round the coast. It must have been in the autumn of 1949, when the leaves from the trees started to make their annual flight into independence and death, that I was first asked if I'd like to join the team. We crept out of the dormitories, Brother Charles having as always given a list of names to the night brothers on dormitory duty so as to let us out, but not without the muffled cries of jealousy from those not allowed to join us, and then, hearts beating, we all met in the back lane beside the school farm.

It was very dark, but he drove only on side lights, and the lorry weaved about the country lanes as we held tight to its sides, since the metal floor was very slippery. After 20 minutes or so we stopped on a cliff above one of the bays. The lights had been doused some time before we arrived at the destination and then with his finger to his lips indicating silence, we followed him down a rough path behind some rocks. After a few minutes he waved his hand for us to crouch down, for he'd seen what we'd come to find. Very dimly visible 100 yards away at the shoreline was a group of dark figures at the edge of the sea, and further away two men in a small boat which was bobbing in the water. My heart was beating and I'm sure the others felt the same excitement as the contraband from the boat was handed to the group on the shore - we were watching smugglers in action.

Our job it seemed was to gather some sort of idea of the amounts of boxes, packets and other objects being handed over. We had to be absolutely still, of course, as to be heard or noticed would have caused at best some sort of attack or aggression, as these smugglers were Breton fishermen bringing in cigarettes and drink, and were risking a great deal in this hazardous trade.

It appears that some 10,000 cigarettes and 50 cases of spirits were handed over that night, for our purposes it seemed was not just to count the contraband, but to report where it subsequently went to. The boat was then pushed out after it was emptied by those on the shore and we heard garbled patois farewells being exchanged. It was time for the men with the goods to start the tedious job of taking all the boxes across the beach and up the cliff path to the waiting van.

Brother Charles had obviously been at this for some time, for he knew where the stuff would arrive, but never when. And so it was that these nightly vigils brought Guernsey and several French fishermen from the Cartaret region of Brittany before the local magistrates in due course.

These hazardous sea journeys of what appeared brave men in hindsight made less than glamorous reading. At the time, cigarettes were in very short supply and in France Gaulois and Gitanes were very cheap and plentiful. Cognac, Cointreau, Benedictine, unavailable things of pre-war luxury, were craved by some in Britain, so a small trade started between France and the Channel Islands in these sought-after items of civilised life. The perpetrators usually got a few weeks inside or were deported if caught, and what then seemed so shady, dangerous and *Treasure Island*-like in its impact on me, was really just small time trading between allies in different parts of the Channel.

The Germans had left in 1945 and in September 1948, when I joined the school and started making those sad journeys away from home, across the stretch from Sark to Saint Peter Port, much of their presence on the islands had disappeared. There were, of course, all the hideouts built into the cliffs and the underground hospital, but of the posters, placards on walls and shop fronts, all these were torn down and burnt very soon after they had left. What had not gone was far more exciting for a boy of nine years old, and formed one of the most adventurous parts of my early life. Brother Charles had discovered, and had kept secret, a cache of hidden German arms. In one cave, guns, pistols, bayonets, swords, emblems, flags, and insignia of every type had been found behind a beautifully disguised, imitation rock, hinged and made to fit exactly in front of the entrance of a cave in a very quiet bay, under an overhanging cliff.

This secret discovery, made by a German speaking islander who had overheard a conversation at the docks just before the occupying forces had left hastily to return to France, was passed on to Brother Charles, who had a knack of being the confidant of many. I'm sure that the Christian Brothers' calling was a hollow life for this swashbuckler who was just like us, a boy at heart.

I had not known initially about this arms find and found out only by a blabbermouth talking, after a friend of his was asked to go and see, but not him. Piqued, he let on to one or two of us, and thereby incurred the full wrath of Bro' Charles. The boy in question who'd given the show away wore the stripe marks on his hands and backsides for days and bandages were needed for the pummelling his body received. He had not let it be known where the cave with the false boulder in front was, as he didn't know, but it made the excitement, now that it was known about, impossible to contain, and the whole thing, even for the select few of Charles' trusties was dropped. This poor fellow then found himself at the receiving end of kicks and blows administered after lights out for preventing this prize 'boys-own' drama from being enacted.

Bro' Charles, like all the others, was called by the shortened form of address, except when a boy was being punished, at which moment it was not allowed to shorten this title even in supplication. This order formed to specialise in the tilling of the soil to emulate Jesus' pastoral and rural image, were outstanding cowherds, butter makers and producers of honey, but as far as I was concerned and judging by the results, were not the cream of the teaching profession.

The temptation was too great for such as Bro' Charles to resist, and it seeped into the daily knowledge of the unsaid that he would like to pick a crew to join him in the lorry in a few days time, to examine the cave. This possibility held captive all our imaginative powers from the first we heard of it.

Intense was the competition within the coterie of 'probables' vying for his favour; sycophancy knew no bounds. My plan, however, was to act as though it didn't matter, as though not to be asked along wouldn't hurt. The question was how to appear uninterested, but also to be asked for this most sought-after sortie. My evolving plan was to ask open, simple questions of the favourite of the bunch likely to go when Charles was not around, like: "Where do you think the cave is?" or "If you are asked what would you most want to get for yourself: a gun, knife, or bayonet?" This particular boy was, however, far too concerned with keeping his mind on the matter at hand, which was to have Bro' Charles constantly aware of his presence, to care about minors' questions.

One evening, the rumour went round that there was to be a meeting to decide the six boys to go. Usually for trips with him Brother Charles would take about 12 or 15 of us, and when it was discovered that only six of us would be picked, my hopes, rightly as it turned out, faded. The day arrived that the six were announced, most of them his closest confidants, not, sadly, including me. They were to leave after lights out and they should each bring a torch. When they got back about eleven p.m. we were all asleep and as none of them who had been were in my dormitory, I had to wait until the morning for the news of the trip. It transpired that it was not an exaggeration; the rumours were true: The cave was indeed full to bursting with armaments of all kinds. The half dozen boys and Bro' Charles had had a job pulling back the imitation boulder, as it had not been opened for some time, and at night darkness made it more difficult. It was absolutely illegal not to declare arms discoveries after the war, and in addition to this the overriding concern for Bro' Charles was the explosive gas inside the cave, for there were gas cannisters there that might be triggered by a boy bringing matches. This fear of explosion shortly had terrible consequences, but for the first foray the boys safely followed Charles.

Those who went there brought back booty which made our impressionable eyes stare: beautifully made daggers with the Iron Cross inlaid in the handles; Luger pistols and leather cartridge holders complete with bullets; sub machine guns; bayonets and ceremonial swords; officers uniforms; helmets and the awful S.S. death's head insignia were all displayed in the dormitories. These articles created such wonderment in the eyes of most of us that the pressure was then unleashed to get either one of the boys (sworn to secrecy) to tell us where the cave was, or to persuade Bro' Charles to take another group.

The days went by. No one would let on, Bro' Charles became quiet and less approachable, and little by little the whole ambiance of the college seemed to change. To those still mad keen to make this journey to get some of the prizes for themselves, hope began to fade. And then the thing happened that, I suppose, Bro' Charles had always feared: one of the original six mentioned at a moment of indiscretion, when showing his Luger to some excited onlookers, that the cave was to be found on the south west tip of the island and that the boulder could be prised back only by pulling from about half way up it on the right hand side facing it.

This was my moment. I knew the boy whom he had told, who then confided in me and without waiting any longer the two of us vowed to creep out that night without permission. We had a torch each and had to creep out past the night duty master down the main staircase and through a window by the front door which was locked, the key being with the night janitor. We had to leave it very late as at night conversations were in progress often until nine p.m. or later, with the topic often that about which we now could wait no longer in discovering for ourselves.

Of course we had to walk, that was the only way, and it took one and a half hours to clamber down the rough path to the beach at the sides of which the caves were to be found. This particular cave was soon seen in front of which the roundish boulder was to be found under a windy moonscape and trembling with nerves, cold, fear and blissful excitement, we heaved at the retaining facsimile and there before our torchlit eyes was an arsenal for our taking. We had agreed between ourselves, Taylor and I, that we would not be greedy and would each take only a representative selection. The cave held a mountain of weapons and the slightly gassy, greasy smell of this enclosed space made it also very frightening. Thinking of its original purpose, I wanted to make my choice and get out back to the college and bed. Taylor felt the same, and with a Luger, bayonet, dagger, helmet and ceremonial sword each we left. We pushed back the boulder and ran, clutching our booty to us closely all the way back with a couple of breach loaders, back through the window still slightly ajar, up past the snoring night duty brother and putting the weapons very quietly beneath our mattresses, we had successfully completed the whole enterprise without being noticed.

A few weeks later tragedy struck. Two boys from the school ignored the warnings about gas and struck matches on entering the cave, so blowing themselves up and with it the dump (which the authorities still didn't know about) and injured several who were still outside. The scandal that broke out over the arms dump and how a Christian Brother from one of the best schools in the Channel Islands could let his pupils see and not report this find, caused him, the school, parents, boys and the authorities the greatest amount of trouble.

The boys had long since hidden their treasures and in my case to this day cannot remember exactly where under the palm tree in our garden in Sark I secreted mine. I feel like Jim in *Treasure Island* when I remember back to those dark nights on the island, when the stuff off dreams was made reality. I'd hidden my treasures there at dusk I remember, before I left for another term at Vauxblets the following day.

Les Vauxblets, now a carpet warehouse, was eventually closed as a school when non-Catholics heavily outnumbered the original Catholics as pupils. It is a dark red building set in fine and extensive grounds with the small shell chapel a place of interest. At Easter we would take it in turns to light candles in the little windows and ledges inside and a priest was on hand to say Mass occasionally so that from outside on autumn days the flickering of the candlelight through the windows from afar made a haunting impression as the light was reflected from off the millions of shells inside. At the little shop not far from the College gates I would spend my 6d a week on condensed milk, which I loved, perforating the small tins with two holes, one opposite the other, and pull hard on the solid liquid from inside. I would have to save up for some time for these tins, but when I'd scraped the money together it would be a great treat going to the shop.

The tuck shop had its opening hours at the school half an hour at lunch time and in the evenings before benediction, a daily event, and I would sometimes, if not saving for the condensed milk, spend it on Aero chocolate.

The result of my time at the Vauxblets was a grounding in teaching at an impressionable age as being a take it or leave it affair with the two extremes of severe physical punishment for even minor infractions, vindictiveness from unfulfilled men who maintained a position somewhere between the lay and the ordained members of their religion and the totally lax attitudes of heroes like Brother Charles, a man for all boys of adventure but not for the history student. At least not for those waverers amongst us, those who find the temptation to fool about, run rings around weaker purveyors of knowledge, and those whose sense of an open opportunity for freedom from scholastic constriction too much to miss. My time there came to an end in 1950, and apart from a short break at home after we had left the Channel Islands for good to settle in Chelsea, my education, so-called, in Sark and Guernsey was over.

CHAPTER 4

CHELSEA

– And my later childhood

In the dark studio again in between houses I spent the winter meeting lots of interesting people, friends of my parents. There was Peter Ustinov who lived up the road, who always said hallo to me; Quentin Crisp and his brightness often seemed nearby. This was just an interlude, for although my father taught at the Westminster School of Art and had exhibited at the Royal Academy, it was his writing that occupied a lot of his time, although poetry-writing, painting and the drawings of all sorts came unhesitatingly from his imaginings. This time in Chelsea was a remaking of friendships and acquaintances after the period spent in Sark.

My brother and I were often asked to go to parties at friends of my parents, who had children of similar ages. Moist sandwiches, egg and cress, thinly sliced cheese, or ham, lettuce and cucumber, under muslin on silver trays, sometimes even staff serving them. The Countess of Moray, a friend of my parents, would ask us to her house in Ebury Street or her other place in Hans Crescent and we would meet Augustus John, Dylan Thomas, Graham Greene or Rodney Ackland; the list went on and on. Later in my boyhood, until I was sixteen or so, I would ask my father to keep the letters of famous people who wrote to him, so I could save them. Because of this, he kept a wonderful letter book for me, into which I pasted the signatures of famous people. In some cases, if the letters were short, he would paste the whole letter. Orson Welles, Alec Guinness, Edith Evans, Laurence Olivier, Stephen Spender, Walter de la Mare, Dylan Thomas, Anthony Quayle: all wrote encouragingly, sometimes ecstatically, of his *Titus* books, or his poems, or both. Without my knowing it, he made a full

Sebastian, Circa 1951

book collection of these names and presented it to me on one of my birthdays. Once I lent it to someone to look at, who cut out Dylan Thomas' signature and later gave it back to someone else, who in turn gave it back to me. Otherwise, it is intact. Under each signature or letter, my father wrote the name, just in case I couldn't read the original. At the time I saw it as a little book for me which he had time to assemble for me. These were just people writing to him, who all admired his work. Only later did I realise that this was something unique and rare; only then did I appreciate the significance of the names which he had collected, not all of whom I knew.

Later, writers like Michael Moorcock, J.G. Ballard, and the poet Michael Horowitz attended the parties given by my parents. The art critic Edwin Mullins; the Oriental specialist of an older generation, John Brophy and his daughter Bridget, were all frequent visitors. In a way, looking at those parties from far off, they left me with a grounding in the language of writers that I can't now do without. I think the atmosphere was generated a great deal by the host and hostess, the ability to listen and to encourage, and the total lack of cleverness, the absence of the gratuitous non sequiturs.

My father had a collection of coats, including a marvellous camel hair one from China. It really was made from camel hide, it smelt, had holes in it and was completely hideous, but was utterly rare. He also had African chiefs' capes, Spanish capes and a great dark blue cape with a brass buckle and pink silk lining. With this on and his lone earring, worn before it became fashionable, my father attracted attention, sometimes indeed provoking aggressive, physical combat and accusations of being homosexual. A more unlikely condition than the last cannot be imagined. I do not know the number of female admirers my father had, but if the line of women I shook hands with recently after a lecture on him is anything to go by, then homosexual he certainly was not. In flowing cape, dark hair brushed back, odd coloured socks, often striding, a handsome, talented young artist, the world of his youth, wherever he was, must have been his oyster. His great array of capes and coats, jerkins and leather jackets, corduroy suits, were all worn with marvellous abandon, as a true original. I emulated him later but much less daringly, being far more conservative, and with a nauseating self-awareness that he did not possess. I wore trench coats which, although worn by Americans, Frenchmen and Italians were still not worn by their originators, the British – or at least the trenchcoat still did not capture the romance that the European brings to it.

I don't think my father had any real enemies. Apart from the mad woman of Chelsea, who put the cheese wire across their front door at throat level, luckily noticed in time, I know of no circumstance in which enmities were made. My father was a taciturn man. As an artist, he knew a lot of the intense feelings that arguments provoked. He knew when the argument was in full swing, that if opposite views prevailed, to join one side or other might lead to physical confrontation, and these often took place in Soho bars, as painters argued different points – bloodied noses, broken arms. Rubens or Delacroix, Matisse or Renoir, Giacometti or Klee: was the fight worth it? He thought not, unless there was real conviction, unless in a way total honour depended on it. From the colourful, spontaneous, histrionic exhibitionism of many of these arguments he fought, you might say, shy. I cannot always maintain his distance. For instance, I maintain that the heroism of the fighters in the Warsaw Ghetto, cooped up in rat-infested sewers, as their city crumbled about them, when they went on and on, as did the partisans in Primo Levi's *If Not Now When?*, this represents some of the greatest acts of exemplary courage in history. On mentioning this to a German friend once, and a Russian on another occasion, and being told that in their opinion the Poles were fools, I would in this case defend my corner to a point at which, if emnity ensued, then that emnity provoked was the concommitant of belief. One of the main reasons for not having had any enemies, I think, was that my father worked best within the family, learning of its workings and thereby knew much more about his wife, children and home than would have been the case if he had gone out to work in the normal way. He taught life painting and drawing at the Royal Academy Schools, the Central School and other institutions, but at all other times he worked from his own home. He has always been something of an unknown figure, for all his fame with his *Titus* books, his *Glassblowers* poems, his illustrations of many of the classics, his plays and drawings, oil paintings and talents as a teacher. This ignorance of him as a man, apart from the establishment's bumbling ineptness in accepting him, instead of ignoring him in their gauche, "We don't know where to place him" excuses, is due in great part to the fact that his huge outpourings took an enormous amount of the short time he had on earth. When in due course the Aladdin's cave of his genius is opened and the coy and the uncommitted venture in, brave enough to find that they haven't been bitten in the process, they will exclaim: "This Mervyn Peake - of course we have always known about him, always was my favourite illustrator".

I'd like to write about my mother now. Mother. What a small word to contain the essence of man. My love of personal apartheid, or, more prosaically put, distance from human involvement, stems in large measure from her. It wasn't, of course, that the person she was with smelt, or whatever, or even that there was a profoundly off-putting aspect to their nature, but that the close proximity of someone else simply provokes a need for attention. The problem gets, as it were, out of hand, as in my case, when I feel that I am set apart. The way a guest holds his knife, if at the same time the conversation in progress involved the deepest of examinations of the first few bars of the Fourth Movement of Mahler's Ninth Symphony and their presaging imminent war, should not matter, but it does. Its mattering, however skillfully argued, lies at a most primitive level of prejudice and cannot, I think, be avoided. Prejudice it is and remains. My mother would not say a word about it, but a woman who had made no obvious effort to make the best of herself and was a guest, or had been met at a party or on introduction, did not receive the immediate attention a well dressed female would elicit.

Mummy, and later Mum, could be the only appellations I ever used, although I would have found it pretty hard to say Mummy in company and didn't ever say it from my fifteenth or sixteenth birthday on. If, on Sark I was naughty or had misbehaved - a daily occurrence - she would ask me to go up to her bedroom when my father was away teaching and would whack me with her hairbrush, either on the hand or bottom: it really stung and sometimes she would be so angry I would be given the full treatment: hand and bottom. Off I would go again, apparently contrite and reformed, back to tantalising something or other, someone or other, until the next time I was caught. Earlier I spoke of her dress sense and her predilection for clothes. Very often I would watch her dressing, putting on make-up or choosing the combinations of things to wear. Certain patterns, as we all know do not go together; nor certain combinations of colour or material; but at the point at which the subtlety of dress sense takes over, a point where many allow a cursory 'That'll do' attitude to guide them, there she would begin to seek a rarer harmony. This called for an expert eye; but then she was a painter and was always fashionable in her appearance. She would never leave her room before feeling right. This 'feeling right', really a need to be noticed, to be admired, was very noticeable throughout her life, and she certainly was noticed. When she entered a room, one felt her presence and this, allied with the fine exploitation of her obvious beauty, made many gasp. She was so obviously in a different class. This quality had another side to it, and if she wasn't noticed, then one fairly soon found out. Her tendency to require compliments once led to my father saying, to my brother and I, that we must always be sure that Mummy is not upset and that we should always treat her well and say how nice she looked. He had a little rhyme, the words of which were changed from the nursery rhyme, and went:

We love little Mummy her coat is so warm

And if we don't hurt her she'll do us no harm.

I remember singing this fairly frequently during my life, from about the age of eight until my early teenage years. For the most part, it was sufficient to notice the way she was dressed, the food was presented, the things she did for the family, but as with most people. Her humour was charming, and in a way incongruous in a beautiful woman. She had always told us how, as a girl, she would limp on purpose. My desire to be discovered beaten and bloody in a gutter, and at one stage to orchestrate arguments that could lead to fights, was from the same source: insecurity. It is easy to be clever about this need for recognition as being odd or indescribably juvenile in intent, but I would maintain that her method and mine were just our way of doing the same thing that many others do, but in different ways.

At breakfast my mother would place puffed wheat pieces under her top gum so that they stuck to the inside of her top lip and then, opening her mouth, let out a blood-curdling witch's cackle. The puffed wheat would look as though they were filthy old teeth and complete a face now contorted and made as ugly as possible with the shutting of her eye, into a real witch. This witch's cackle, which she often used at unexpected moments, was very realistic and was when I was younger, quite terrifying. A habit to which she was frequently prone was of asking for a number from one to ten, and then going off into her own thoughts. The particular number given then translated the letters from A to J. After switching off after, say, the letter C was given, she would metaphorically disappear leaving us to our own thoughts. Now, years after her premature death, these idiosyncracies seem isolated and divorced from them when they happened almost daily.

She had a range of little tricks to play on us. At meal times she would sometimes hand over our plates after serving the food with just one pea on the plate, or would give us coffee in dolls' house cups and be absolutely serious about it, as the look on her face showed. The others, after having asked permission, would begin to eat, those with normal helpings, while the person with the tiny helping would have to wait. We would then all burst out laughing and she would let the sufferer of the day have their food. One certainly couldn't have got annoyed, even when famished. That would not have been accepted and usually it <u>was</u> great fun. Only when it went on for too long did it pall, although any hint of its irritating us would have caused her to change her mood and she might say "Don't you like my little joke?" "Of course, Mummy." Lots of these sort of things were in her repertoire, like placing things at the very edge of tables so they looked as though they would fall off, or wearing a collapsible top hat and holding a cane as she did a magnificent interpretation of a Marlene Dietrich sexy song in German. My mother spoke German, so the authenticity of the 'Lili Marlene' song or 'Ich bin von kopf biss fuss auf liebe eingestellt' ('Falling in love again') came across wonderfully, as she slowly danced on our famous Sark pine table after lunch and the dishes had been cleared away. She was not an ordinary mother, she was my mother, and had qualities that emerged because they were uniquely hers. My father's catalytic and singular influence gave her the moment and the security to expand from the shy cocoon of an Irish Catholic upbringing into the wholly original woman that she became. She loved my father with a partisan fanaticism with which a genius is sometimes rewarded.

'... Into the sculpture room he came, quick and sudden and dark, and when he left the room they said, "That's Mervyn Peake; he's dying of consumption." For me, at seventeen, someone dying of consumption (even though he was not) had a terrible romance about it!' So begins my mother's book of her life with my father and *A World Away* traces her life with him from that young age to his death in 1968. She ends: 'You have gone. I long to see you again.' Her book, published and written within only a year of his death, is a *tour de force* in its romantic tragedy and is tender and loving, perceptive and quiet, as well as being a controlled display of what human dignity is able to achieve. The display of grief by Wagner's widow at the graveside is surely what my mother felt; so, probably, did many wives of the uniquely talented. Somehow, the prerequisite control was achieved and my mother went on after his death to make sure she did everything she could to advance his reputation. In the 1970's, when his book sales were fairly low, when the discovery had not yet been made of his contribution to illustrate classics, his poetry for the most part unread, she went on and on and in a very solitary way. It is this mission that I see as my life's work as well. One day, when the wider reading public becomes aware of his talents and not just the imaginative and sensitive ten per cent, her work (and my continuation of it) will be vindicated.

Just after I was born I was photographed by my father with Polyphoto, which at that time was a very new method of photography and usually used for baby bubbling and dolled up in party best, propped against cushions, possibly smiling. I was photographed in a series of 100 pictures in all manner of nude relaxation. 'Sebastian at 10 days' this group was called, and he suggested that a black cloth be laid out on the studio floor and that I should just move about freely. Some of the shots show that if he had been interested in the subject he could have been a good photographer. These pictures, and the many many taken by my parents, began a collection of albums which in the end contains snaps and composed photographs that spanned the one taken just after I was born in 1940 through my mother's early years to my records of my sister. Some taken by my mother on Sark at the grand fancy dress competition held in 1948 especially for the then Princess Elizabeth's visit to the island, beautifully capture the exotic apparel designed and put together by my father. I spoke of the day earlier in this story and my waiter to Fabian's clown is a case in point. It was not just an instant composite but brought out the hopes for success in those boys' faces.

My mother had a habit, which unfortunately I have inherited, of gripping the thumbs in the palms of her hands, or pressing different fingers into contortions that brought the white to the surface. A need to cling onto security perhaps, but one I think I make a more conscious effort to eradicate than she did. Trailing my arm outside my bed in hot weather to achieve a coolness, would only be feasible for a second or so, because I always felt that someone was going to come from somewhere and touch or grip my hand. I am not sure if there is a connection between the gripping of my thumb and a feeling of fear at being touched by the unknown other hand, but a feeling persists.

The short stories that she wrote, observations of the way that people behave to each other, often unaware of the effects they have on others, were acutely seen through a gifted eye. These stories, which are unpublished, show how much we are unaware that a change takes place when one person says something to another whose experience of life is different; thus both people, although speaking the same language, hear different things, different meanings, and as Louis MacNeice observed 'Two people with one pulse'. This would have been her goal.

CHAPTER 5

KENT

– A Georgian House amidst the hops and orchards

Our next house, in Smarden in Kent, a Georgian manor house, had proportions of great beauty, with columns outside, long sash windows and a vast greenhouse to one side. It had a pond with fish and an apple orchard of over an acre. As I was eleven years old and had already lived in six houses, I was getting quite used to moving about with my parents. The nomadic life already lay in my character.

My next school, the local village one, does not impress itself greatly on my memory, perhaps as my short time there was less than a year. Perhaps the most exciting event of our time in Kent was the arrival of the Peake's first car. An engineer friend of my parents made its delivery one day. He had a very pretty daughter, taller than me by a foot, who once, when I met her in our years in Chelsea, used some wildly bad language, which both shocked and fascinated me. Now she accompanied her father when he secretly delivered our car. For my parents to own a car was like me taking a post in pure maths at a university, so when, on the day after I'd arrived home, I was led blindfolded to the garage by a small family group, I was quaking with excitement.

The door was opened to reveal what would now be a collector's piece: a 1936 Wolsey with bonnet temperature gauge, sun roof and wire wheels, and with the engineer, his daughter and my mother and father looking on, I smiled and said "Cor! Terrific, a car!" My father could never hold secrets, but bizarrely thought I could put it from my mind if he **hinted** at something. He had vaguely mentioned a Wolsey, and the idea had been going around in my head like the whirl of dervishes ever since that hint was let loose. At the time, *Fabian of the Yard* and most other British police stories on film featured the chases using the Wolsey 6/80, a mighty, usually black painted powerful car that had, for its time, a most modern and lovely shape. But the Wolsey that arrived was nothing like a 6/80: this was the rural midwife's car, the old gentleman's carriage. Inside my heart gasped in dismay, but outwardly I grinned with boyish pleasure and I hoped I hadn't given the show away.

At the same time, Victoria, the engineer's daughter, made her entrance into my own growing awareness of womens' pull over me. Unfortunately she and her father didn't stay after they had delivered the old romantic car, but left immediately. The impression she made was not so much of her as an actual person, for she was older and I didn't know her, but of the tempting lure of which I'm sure she was unaware; that opposite that seems magnetic.

In the apple orchard, my parents' beloved cat had a hole in one of the bigger trees in which it would sit attempting to snap at, and always miss, the birds perching in the branches above. Chlöe had been with us through five moves and even in Kent at ten years old she still had a long life left, until the last pathetic attempt to climb the stairs in a future house brought her tumbling down, the strength having given out. She died while on her way to the airing cupboard on the first floor, her favourite spot.

Gypsies sometimes parked their caravans at the end of the orchard beyond our land and were often moved on. Occasionally they stayed for a few weeks and the wooden, highly coloured, horse drawn vehicles were visible through the trees in the Spring before the leaves were fully out on the apple trees. Once I went with the wife of the leader of the band of wanderers and some of their children blackberrying in a local wood. The Romany dialect was still very much in use and at the times of hop picking, apple or potato harvesting, they made some cash labouring for local farmers. This blackberrying was on a day off for them, so I joined them. A rather more unpleasant part of that rural afternoon came about when the gypsy woman in question said that she "wanted a shit", lifted up her skirt and did just that. No under garments needed to be removed, she had none. This rather displeasing interlude, from which I stole away, did make me very aware that the gypsies at the bottom of the garden had quite different habits from ours. I don't think a self respecting Romany would lure an innocent from the house to go blackberrying just to shock. It seems that she just was not used to the sanitized ways of others. Her appearance was alarming. She was beefy, with a wild eye and a powerful voice. If at closing time, or even approaching it, she peered through the public bar window (this being before the 'No Travellers' signs were put up), and saw her husband reeling about singing too loudly or in any way misbehaving, she would punch him heftily and drag him out, back to the gaily painted but grubby interiors of their caravan.

There was a very old lady in the village who made things for my mother to give as presents on birthdays and Christmas and Easter holidays, things like jumpers, knitted skirts and gloves. She lived just on the outskirts of the village in an ancient cottage that had no electricity inside, water or lavatory and certainly no bathroom, near a reed inlet which was home to moorhens and coots. She always reminded me of a witch, but was a knitter of the first order. When sent to collect whatever she had finished, I liked to leave quickly. Although she was only an old lady and allegedly harmless, the long long fingers and the black fingernails which completed the ends of her bony arms always caught my breath. One dusk, arriving for a collection I walked up her path, the flickering candle visible through the tiny window at one side of the front door, and I heard whispering coming from the little reed bed opposite. I felt terrified and only stayed a moment or so, thanking her for her lovely work as quickly as I could and wished her goodnight. There was not a sound as I left and I ran home the half a mile or so with my heart pumping. I discovered later that the same gypsies set traps for ducks and other water birds often found in this slightly marshy land.

Like many boys, I was fascinated when crime came to the village. A celebrated murder happened in Smarden in the early 1950's when a local girl was murdered, then discovered some days later by frogmen who dredged the village pond. A local man, himself thought 'odd' by the villagers, was apprehended and was tried for murder, but because of his state of mind he was sent to Broadmoor. In retrospect this is horrifying but it captivated me then. During the dredging, the local village school was shut as the pond was adjacent to it, so we had time off which pleased me even more. This school gave the first public performance of my father's play *The Wit to Woo*, which was later so badly received in London. At the village school the one production that was put on was an immense success. The locals clapped, and at the end I stood up and in a clear penetrating voice announced, "My father wrote that play!" I felt great pride, though now I feel a kind of embarrassment. "That's interesting," some said to me or "I know he did, his name is on the front of the programme," all in an amiable tone and a far cry from the public and humiliating panning the London critics gave it later. In time it was vindicated by Laurence Olivier's letter that says that he'd 'just read your exciting and highly original play that Vivien (Leigh) and I would like to do'. They didn't, unfortunately, but so much of his work was far too good and far ahead of its time.

I was now ready for senior school. Had we stayed in the Channel Islands I might have gone to the senior part of Vauxblets, but having moved back to England, another Christian brothers' establishment was sought for me to attend. The nearest, Mayfield College, was only 20 miles away. I had got used to being a day boy for the time we were in London and couldn't bear the thought of yet another boarding school, especially of this kind. Mayfield College reminded me of Colditz, stark, red brick, in a hollow and facing wooded, undulating land which sloped away, down to the playing fields and to the permanently dirty and slime covered swimming pool. They gave it a wash and brush up once a term.

The news that I was going away again I took with a sinking heart, and I implored, cajoled and almost broke down over not being sent away again. It was no avail, to Mayfield College I went. I remember hating the place, loathing the smell of the place, its situation, the people I saw, the study, my classroom and so it was that from 1952 to 1954 I attended another establishment I vowed would get nothing from me. The more the scholastic discipline demanded of me, the more I'd make sure that my talents would not be extracted. To pay the establishment back was the only way I could in any way say, through my policy of disruption, that I hated my being sent away. Shortly after I arrived I'd heard that if you ate soap it would make you ill, which was what I wanted, as it would be time off in the sanatorium. I ate as much as I could find - a bar of Wrights coal tar soap, the school issue - and really was ill, and for two weeks I enjoyed life in the lovely clear, crisp sheets of the sanatorium, and matron's full attention, as I played the charming boy who had seen the stupidity of his ways.

War books were inescapable then. *The Colditz Story*, *The White Rabbit*, *The Dambusters* – all were very popular and I read them in the comfort of my bed. I did get better, unfortunately, and it was then back to the dormitory, the daily morning mass and evening benediction. Only occasionally was I bullied. Once I was tied hand and foot to a revolving blackboard and bombarded with chalk, dusters and missiles of all kinds for being called Sebastian, so I could suck up to the said religious master. "Repent for being called by that name," the leader of the group said. "I repent," I answered quickly. At least at that moment it was true - I really did regret it. With blood drawn from face and neck, I was undone and let loose. I was never able to organise my retribution on that boy, he seemed invulnerable and had a posse round him always. I paid the price and was left alone.

I'm far more interested in the individual and his ability to say something I want to hear or feel towards than the sweaty endeavours of lots of people all wanting the same thing. But about this time I had to join teams, for at Mayfield like everywhere else, the school had their Blue Team and their Red Team and whatever else they thought up; I had to play cricket and rugby most weeks at the appropriate times of the year for these sports and my first thought was how I could get out of these games and still be seen as honourable.

The first winter term at Mayfield I had to see the lie of the land vis-a-vis rugby and its attendant grime and at least have a bash at appearing *sportif*. I'd run madly around hoping to look willing to try to catch the ball at least, or appear to be helping my side along. After a few weeks of getting mud all over me for what seemed to me a completely dubious purpose, I worked out a knack of running like mad in the general direction of the pack towards whatever end they were heading for. By so doing, if the charge was on the wooded side of the pitch, I could disappear into the trees and not even be missed. Naturally I didn't want to be found out, that wouldn't have seemed to be playing the game, so I dropped back in again the next time they all were to be found heaving, panting and puffing away on the wooded side again a quarter of an hour later. In this way rugby days were spent running up and down looking busy on the open side for most of the time, and the rest of the match was spent watching muddy bodies getting pummelled and bashed about from the wooded side of the pitch.

In the summer term we went after school down the long sloping field towards the filthy swimming pool which, as I mentioned before was usually very dirty and badly looked after, but at the beginning of term it got pretty crowded for it was clean. We would usually not have an attendant or supervisor after school and some of the boys would have cigarettes that they would secrete in their towels that we would puff away at or taking turns when only one was available. Talk was of how to get more cigarettes, the inevitable dirty jokes, girl talk. I took it all in, but only contributed usually to subjects like how to disrupt classes by humming or tapping under desks, or with completely incapable teachers, how to ask very provocative questions deliberately to embarrass them. I seemed to have the knack of never getting caught and some of my schoolmates would ask how I did it. I did it by making noises, coughing suddenly and extremely loudly when the brother's back was turned, so he would practically jump out of his skin but could not identify a culprit. I also persuaded a whole group of the class to say in unison, from different parts of the classroom, "He did sir!", so that for a split second the master thought that someone was actually owning up or treacherously pointing the finger at the boy concerned. Another trick: on being asked a question I would put my hand up and put on an awful stutter on the first letter of the answer, then change the answer to, "Could I be excused sir?"

All this was passed on to my parents when I saw them at half term or terms' end, but I think behind the scenes I was to remain there by hook or by crook. I hadn't quite left the school for good when a notice went up, that a school in the East End of London had been asked to present a boxing tournament between their chosen fighters, and volunteers were asked for at the College. I volunteered I think, or was made to feel that I'd be good at it, so I did. Very nervous underneath about the whole thing, while feigning enthusiasm, I did some training with punch bags and some sparring partners. I suppose they thought after a few weeks that I'd be alright on the night, and as the first of the two nights over which all the matches were to be held approached, I felt quite confident about the prospect. There were to be twelve bouts on the first evening, with two bouts in each weight. I was the flyweight. My opponent, who came from Clapham, spoke with a broad nasal cockney accent. We were the first match of the evening. The winner of the first evening would fight the second six who had won the night before.

The night arrived, and as the lights went down in the hall, we climbed into the ring. The bell went for the first of three by three minute rounds. I came out fighting, and this Clapham boy Williams got a real bash on the nose fairly early on, but apart from that punch my role was one of sparring, deflecting, and a bit of holding. As our fight was the first of the evening, I knew that if I won this one I could step out and know that that was my contribution for the evening. The Londoners thought they were in a very posh place and naturally put on imitiation loud, snobby accents which didn't quite come off and used this and other jokes to try to warm up the atmosphere for the coming tournament. The second round he hit me somewhat harder but without a good aim. Then I saw an opportunity and let fly with what I had to offer against his solar plexus. This last seemed to do the trick for as the round was nearly at an end and he looked winded, the referee stopped the contest and I was declared the winner. My right hand held aloft, "The blue corner has it," he shouted to the cheering of Mayfield and the booing of London. So there it was, this mini gladiator, of getting on for six minutes' experience, lighted by the floodlights, led out to the shower, clapping my opponent on the back when we met outside, I felt my day had come. In the end it was six all the first evening, so the tie was the starting score for the second evening. My opponent in the red corner this time was an Italian called Manzini, an Eastender of unsmiling and quite unflappable disposition, or so he seemed. Again we were the first contest being the lightest, and into the ring we went. Eyeing each other across the ring, listening to the advice from our respective corners about the honour of our respective sides, gumshields in, laces checked at the gloves, sawdust for the boots, spitoon for the breaks, we attacked each other. Manzini came at me, I deflected. I'd beaten Williams, I'd do the same again: a punch to the jaw. I was still thinking of the previous night's victory, being seen as a hero, hard into the stomach came the next blow, deflection - the bell.

This was not my cup of tea; the second bell, and out came this Italian with fire, and the same thoughts in his soul as mine, with one glancing crash he broke the bridge of my nose and profuse bleeding came forth down my nose. I'd had enough, the second bell had not been rung but that would do me I thought, humiliation openly to see, and with the blood streaming down, I walked across the ring, lifted the ropes and left the hall, to the surprise of a flabbergasted Manzini, the seconds, the timekeeper and the whole school. As it happens, it didn't concern me what people thought and when I think back to this very strange occurrence and how I coped with public humiliation I feel that my justification is that it was the right thing to do at the time. Naturally one wouldn't brag about giving up in such circumstances, but it was not held against me.

Mayfield College had a separate girls' establishment in the same village and rumour had it that nightly dormitory visits were made; this information I found highly tempting, and wanted to get myself involved, but I was only twelve years old, uninitiated, green, and certainly not tall enough to scale the great outer walls, all of which militated against experimenting with a subject that was slowly but surely taking over in rank of importance. In any case, at this moment the time had come to leave not only Mayfield but also Smarden too, for the beautiful house had been unfortunately beyond the financial means of my parents to keep up, and so we went back to London for a while.

My parents still had the lease on the Manresa Road Studio at the time and my father would use the place as a very useful *pied à terre* when earlier over from Sark and later from Smarden. Right in the middle of Chelsea, the road ran due north-south from the colourful Kings Road end, with its Georgian houses, to the Kensington end and the Fulham Road. The Queen's Elm pub where many writers and painters went, was at hand, just around the corner but he didn't ever drink there – at least I never saw him do so, except a glass of cherry brandy once at Christmas.

The studio, with one enormous north light, the great 40 foot high ceiling and the smell of turps, oil paint and charcoal of the painter's refuge, this was home once again for my nomadic family. There were five of us, and my sister born on Sark and brought into the world by my grandfather like myself, was now about three years old. At this time between schools I was at home like my sister, but my brother, not old enough for changing to a senior school still attended preparatory school. So here we all lived for a while, six months or so, until the arrangements were made for selling Smarden, that wonderful house. We were sad to leave and not all that keen to move into the Surrey suburbs, which were to be our next destination.

CHAPTER 6

WALLINGTON IN THE SOUTHERN SUBURBS

– Where someone said of one of my father's
best oil paintings: "That's funny, I dabble too"!

The move to Wallington, Surrey, came about with dispiriting speed, and the Smarden house was, sadly, sold back to the bank from which the loan for its purchase had been taken out in the first place.

When my grandfather had retired from medical work in China, he had had built a large house in which he would have his surgery. His nurse lived in and until she died, his wife ran this Victorian Gothic house, a house into which we were now going to move. There were six bedrooms, a very large garden, a tennis court, a mosaic tiled conservatory and a half moon drive with great wide cross and bar gates at either side of the frontage. The local bus which was to take me to my next school every day stopped at the request stop just outside one of the gates, under a great oak tree, and later on my job was to weekly clear hundreds of bus tickets, sweet papers and detritus of every kind stuffed into our hedge or just thrown into our drive. Once when no one was looking my father stuck a ten shilling note to the pavement with very strong glue. We would then watch from a window that gave a view of the bus stop the wary attempts to pick it up. People would sometimes kneel down pretending to be doing up their shoe laces but really trying to prise the note from its grip. Others would openly bend down and try to get their finger nails underneath it; all manner of methods - surreptitious, furtive, open - were used, but the note held firm and a week later at a quiet time of the day, my father got a thin blade and slicing under the note from one side to the other, retrieved his money. He had several money tricks. He could flick coins up his sleeve with great dexterity and we children never could work out how the coins could so easily disappear if his shirt sleeves or jumper were not loose. Another, more vocal, trick won my complete admiration: his ability to belch through the alphabet was a magnificent feat, one it took us ages to master, although I don't think my sister ever tried.

What a change from the urban colour, the sights and sounds of London, the very quiet rural elegance of the Georgian house in Kent, or the wild brown lanes and cliffs of Sark, was this south London commuter town.

A school had been found for me to attend, this time run by fully fledged men of the cloth, priests who had had the ability to pass the Latin exams at their places of instruction, but were nevertheless representatives of the constriction of practical education that is classrooms, rules, hierarchies, masters and power. At least this place was a day school. As the bus stop was just outside our gate and as the journey to school lasted only 15 minutes, this was a wonderful change from the often appallingly rough journeys on the ferry from Weymouth to St Peter Port, or by plane from Blackbush to Guernsey, or the many sad and heart-rending separations at Creux harbour.

The bus journey, on that first morning in 1953 through the leafy roads and the short walk from the main road near the school entrance to the aptly named Peeks Hill, was pleasant. My new uniform bright, crisp and the school emblem on the breast pocket of the dark blue blazer was worn with less of the dislike for which I held the Vauxblets and Mayfield uniforms.

This first day there brought, at least subconsciously, a relief from a naturally fairly destructive attitude to schools. The day school meant that I was where I really only ever wanted to be, at home, where I had my extensive collection of model cars, some pistols, knives and swords I'd been given, valuable old flint boxes - since stolen - and swashbuckling and dangerous, two killer battle swords, all these in my den. I kept my rooms always very tidily and would have displays for friends to see if they came to visit me. That day I did my best to maintain a solid and progressive feel in my inner attitude towards the classroom, masters and schoolmates.

As the days and months went by, this initial fine attitude waned, as awful marks in papers, and no sign of any apparent improvement in my progress, came forward. When I had been there six months or so, and I had been asked so often at home to try to concentrate, to try to be less interested in being disruptive, I think, in a way, I threw in the scholastic towel once and for all.

There was a French teacher who at the beginning of each new term would say that as there had been so much fooling about in the previous term (often due to me) that for this term there would be no repetition of it. "I will not repeat myself, do you hear me laddies? I will not repeat myself." This sentence, in which he never saw the humour, was repeated every term for the years I was at the school and was the sentence immediately prior to his next entreaty that, "Now for dictation laddies and I will not repeat the words." As the dictation was always the same we could prepare missiles for future classes - he was a type of teacher who was at once totally consistent in his repetition but was completely unpredictable as far as violent, physical outbursts were concerned. So although we could be getting prepared for the next poor chap's hell, with the French teacher we had to watch our step. The dictation started with the words we pretended we didn't hear and it was always 'Ve cow', 'Ve 'orse' and the side-splitting 'Ve sparkling plug'. The man, who was Polish and was a prisoner of the Germans for several years during the war, should have been treated with more respect. But if after ten years he still didn't know that it was the 'sparking' and not 'sparkling plug'; still gave the same 10 words he'd always done; said 'Ve' and not 'the' and still did not know that one said 'the horse' and not 'Ve 'orse', then maybe I shouldn't just blame myself for my less than scintillating academic progress.

This propensity towards sound as language, the apeing of sound, the mimicry of the different accents and dialects was as yet some way off and at that time, with the Polish French teacher, my horizons were pretty confined. The gift of the mispronunciation of the French teacher's English, and the vocal problems of the teacher who could not say the letter 'R' (so when a school friend called Rogers got things wrong, the teacher's anger with him, bursting out always with, "Wearly Wogers, can't you get anything wight?" was greeted by unrestrained guffawing) both prompted my involving others in my aim of disrupting the course of the period. After the third or fourth time of hearing, "Wearly Wogers", I repeated it using a technique of appearing as though I agreed that Rogers was an idiot and that I should join the teacher in his admonition. Of course for a second it appeared to the others that I really was siding with the teacher, but after turning round and making a sign that they should join in, they grasped that a great deal of fun was to be had by producing a gradually mounting chant of, "Wearly Rogers, can't you get anything wight?" This inexorably mounting chant finally causing the poor teacher to fetch the tougher Maths master who was in the next door classroom, he came in to complete silence. Remarking, "Well they had been shouting at the tops of their voices before I came for assistance", didn't put him in a very good light as far as anyone was concerned.

This Maths teacher, a nasty looking man, was very short, had rimless glasses and a crew cut and maintained total discipline by meting out strap notes, or 'chits' as they were called then, at the slightest provocation. Provocation to him could be, "Excuse me Father, could you explain that again?" This was either taken as ignorance, or as a questioning of his capacity of making himself quite clear the first time. He chose the absolute opposite approach to teach his subject from the lax or ineffectual ones. His method was the iron grip method and was as inefficient as a way of imparting knowledge for some boys as the opposite was for others. Naturally these different approaches were not based on whims, but the only way in which their personalities were able to be projected or otherwise through teaching. In any case as I don't think I can remember a single one of them from any of the schools that gripped my attention, except Brother Charles, and he only as a man not as a master, it didn't seem to matter at the time.

What I needed, wanted and would have worked hard with was a person who straddled the subject, who radiated his belief and lured me into his grip. He would have needed the ability to root me to the spot, to fire me with his powerful personality. But it was not to be and the days passed at this school were as at any of the others, lost in idleness my mind wandering and waiting in a way for life to begin. At school all I found was the different classrooms with their individual smells, and features, were the daily drudge, the regimed and statutory years of incarceration.

I did a bit of sport; the teams were picked and I liked the idea of the fast bowler. Denis Compton and, somewhat later, Freddie Truman began to appear as heroes in my life, especially Compton, who had a physical presence I could respect, for I needed the man to appear like a larger than life character, someone in whom I could see no flaw, and if he had one, which he like anyone else would have had, it would have been so subservient to the total image of achiever and hero. In his case the flowing dark hair as he tore down the pitch with style, speed and personality, powerfully put into action his ability. For in the singular competence that places the highly talented person apart from the rest lies the lure. Sometimes I'd look for the signs of weakness in the hero, something I could dislike so as to make his achievement less of note, make him in short less distanced through his talent and so become more able to be caught up with, copied, imitatable, someone I might be able to equal – in short, to make the hero my equal.

I got involved in quite a few fights which again I would orchestrate, wanting to prove my worth at something other than fooling and disruption, at which I was second to none. Surreptitiousness was my trade, the art of innuendo, deviousness, implication, and attendant schemes to deflect from commitment or just the real hard work of it all.

Once or twice I went camping, which I loathed; all the mud, grubbiness, the 'team spirit', kettles boiling over, cold nights, hard work and camaraderie was not for me. Pitching tents in wind, finding flat ground, the apparent spirit undaunted, marching on to nowhere, with continual freezing goose pimples, all seemed to me as irrelevance. I joined the Scouts one evening; it was also to be the last evening with them. I tried the morse code explained by someone who seemed uninterested himself in the subject. I asked if I could try out 'Help me please' by making the relevant taps. By the end of the evening I still didn't get what one was supposed to do, feigned a bad stomach, went home and the Scout movement continued on its way without me.

My scouting days being over, the school Army Cadet Corps caught my eye. They met once a week in a hut. This army cadet gathering was run by a very tough corporal who used to drill us and show us weapons, touched as though they were the rarest of objects. One week there was a bren gun which was taken to bits and put back together again. Then next week we would put it together and then dismantle it again. The Corporal would arrive in all weathers half an hour before we all arrived, all seven of us that is, and put in 30 minutes taking each piece out and polishing it, then placing all the component parts along in lines ready for the evening puzzle. As each week he put everything in the same order, we fairly soon got the hang of it.

We were to have polished our boots until they shone like mirrors, the webbing and straps as new and the blancoing perfect, to complete this Army Cadet's dreary uniform. I often wondered why he would polish and expect all of us to spend ages before the evening's drill polishing, only to meet in a hut near the railway station in Purley. It's like the doctors' surgeries or solicitors' front office doors, I felt: this paying the cleaner to polish practically out of sight the brass handle on the door, but at the same time not noticing that the door was practically falling off the hinges, being so rusty. Once inside, some doctors' and solicitors' offices sport naked light bulbs, peeling outdated wallpaper, and provide the honoured clients or patients with dog-eared and scruffy old magazines. The Corporal was like that: he would polish, polish and polish again, but when out of uniform would be seen in shapeless clothes with his elbows sticking very nearly out of the worn out jumpers he wore.

The Cadet period lasted somewhat longer than the Scouts, getting on for a term, and on the day that the annual mock battle came around, held in some woods near Dorking, I was quite excited. Blanks were to be used and we really would be firing at our enemy, the Waddon cadets, from behind trees and from banks in the wood. This was to be the day the Corporal saw as the vindication of his claim that the Purley Cadets were of the competence of the S.A.S. or crack commando battalions at the very least. Poor chap. The day of the battle began with overcast skies that fell as torrential rain by the time we got in the coach taking us to the place of combat. He tore about in the mud, blasting out shots at figures seen fleetingly darting from tree to cover, and from cover to hollows. A draw was declared when we looked like the water buffalo in the Lower Ganges and no-one could tell who was on the Waddon or the Purley side. The great battle between the 8th Army and the Afrika Corps in miniature was over, and filthy, wet, dripping in the pure awfulness of it, this was my last go at soldiering, and back we went to the hut in Purley for a mug of tea.

One day my parents did receive a communication from the Home Office stating that His Majesty's forces would not be requiring my effort for National Service, as being born on the 7th January 1940 I had missed that hell by eight days. If I had had to join I would like to have become involved in some aspect of music. And it was on being asked to put some bamboo sticks in the ground to hold the french beans up straight, that I started my life long interest in drumming. On pressing the stick into the rather hard earth it broke in two and I started tapping it on any flat surface I could find. Meanwhile, the cadets, the scouts, sports, all faded out to be replaced by the slowly mounting intense interest in women and girls. Of course as any other boy, awareness of the more beautiful sex had started by one's awareness of the role of mother and the impact on seeing her as a woman for the first time.

Naturally one's parents would be seen going in and out of the bathroom, and my elegant mother, who had a very attractive shape and slim, well shaped legs, was my yardstick. Sometimes as I was walking past, or early on in the main bedroom of wherever we were living, her elegant and fine female form would be visible through the silken nightclothes she would wear. When I was still very young we had gone over for a short holiday, back to the small hotel in Burpham whilst living in Chelsea. We went out in a party with some people also staying there and their daughter of twenty or so. They took us in their car to Littlehampton beach, and there, while collecting some shells the daughter had an accident with her costume. One of her very ample breasts dropped out. It was very exciting for me, but she quickly put it in her hands and made an attempt to stuff it back into her costume. I don't know why I felt that that small act of replacement should have been handled in any other way, but the period between exposure and being secreted again I suppose was far too short. On another occasion walking up Oxford Street, my mother noticed that the woman ahead of her had her skirt tucked into her knickers. She pointed this out to the woman, who turned aggressively to her and said, "What's it got to do with you, mate?" These two incidents surely show that for some people temporary slips in their physical emplacement are not as important as to others.

It was at this time when at the age of about 13 that

I'd noticed a girl around who seemed to be often in male company, either older boys or grown-ups. I think I must have seen her on buses or walking about on Saturday mornings when the youth of the area would amble up and down the main street talking and arranging parties and things to do in the weekend evenings. She was quite tall, slim and had a good shape; she had long dark hair and was from a large detached house further up the Woodcote Road where I lived. I had found out her house by noting that she would get off the bus a hundred yards or so further up from the bus stop outside our gate and go up the drive to her door. It must have taken some time and observation to notice all this, but plucking up courage one evening when I saw her on her own, I asked if I could take a stroll with her. It wasn't possible that day, but if I would like to see her the best way would be to meet her parents formally since, as I lived in the same road, it would not look like her being just picked up.

So not wanting to, but feeling that to wait a week or so would make me seem less eager, I nodded once or twice from the other side of the road sometimes, but held my beating body in check until I felt she would maybe find me more interesting. The third week after she'd made her offering and having mouthed, "This evening?" across the road, to which she nodded, I walked up to her house. She opened the door to me and took me up to the first floor where her parents were sitting, the father was reading the paper, the mother knitting.

"This is Sebastian," Suzanne said and her father, a solicitor I think, greeted me quite amiably and the mother looked up and nodded. It was the beginning of my life as a man.

● ● ●

This marks, I think, the beginning of the end of my childhood. My childhood is the first part of my life, under the spell of my father; my early adulthood the second part, one in which my life, though completely different, was still ruled by being my father's son.

I was well into my late twenties when I left home literally, rather than metaphorically. Although I had spent some four years abroad after leaving school and tutors, I never felt I'd actually really left. I couldn't. The pull of the atmosphere, the lure of its smell, the essence of home was too strong to give up. Although the years abroad gave me three fluent languages, opportunities to play my drums and piano in jazz clubs all over Europe, and myriad encounters with girls and women, the call of something stronger always seemed to pull me back. All the houses, flats and cottages are now owned by others, all are changed out of all recognition, gone forever into memory. There stalks abroad in those Channel Islands, Kent and Sussex, Chelsea and Kensington houses, a uniqueness that is indestructible, the treasure of being a child of bliss in the Peake household.

On leaving home I left the oils and pencils, the pine table and the green covered Georgian chairs – their only furniture of worth – I left the smell of something dear, precious, untranslatable. A mystery, something to die for, to kill for, to protect, to cherish, to which to remain fearlessly loyal, to revere and be proud of, something which was irreplaceable. At the end of *Gormenghast*, although he is physically walking away, Titus is, I think, walking forwards and backwards at the same time. Away from his home, the castle, his mother the countess; but back to them at the same time. I think of a ship in a great storm that is further back than when the storm broke despite seeming to go forward, for the power of the elements is pulling it back. And this pull, what is it? I don't know, and sometimes I wished it would release me. Why couldn't I have fallen in love and said goodbye smiling and running expectantly into the new? What was/is the hold of that which has gone?

What is the explanation for my feeling which runs deep like the river in *Titus Alone*? A never ending flood going nowhere, coming from nowhere, destined to beat always at the heart's door of those whose insatiable need for love prevents them from seeing what is there before them. Blinded by the illusion of rejection, unjust, in its assumption that the people who produce emotional misfits like me are destined to tramp the same road in one direction as I am in another. Not meeting because a rendezvous is impossible. I do not believe I was loved, although it was patently obvious I was. Like St. Thomas I cannot believe even when I see the holes in Christ's hands. I will end my days and get in the box like everyone else with the absolute conviction that intrinsically I am unlovable. And so on leaving home I aimed like the successful salmon to leap the highest rapids but I was dragged back by the underflow and the pull of the sea, so that, like the unsuccessful salmon, I languished in the shallows.

Moments of adventure, crossing the Sahara, Lapland in summer, being shot at in Lisbon, being cheered in a Bordeaux bar playing African poly-rhythms on a table in a bar to lunchtime break grape pickers or taking my first £1,000 private sale order 20 years ago: these examples of moments of isolated thrill compete with the dream of home but never replace it.

EPILOGUE

My father had a very philosophical attitude to physical pain, and on hitting his thumb hammering, would say nothing. The puce face and the rising colour it caused would, of course, be as painful as it would be for the person who screams out, swears or reacts by throwing the hammer across the room or toolshed. He gave no indication of being in pain and took it all, whether hammer blow, glass cut or simply falling over, as though the event simply had not occurred. He would not shout obscenities, as he did not like to swear, but tried whenever possible, even during particularly trying times with wife or children, to keep his outbursts to something harmless. The most violent utterance I can ever remember was the expletive 'Jehozaphat'.

Towards the final years of his life, he could not make his speech understood. His pathetic slurrings of the voice were incomprehensible. The years of institutional care took their toll on his mind, for he could lash out, physically and verbally at the nearest thing in sudden frustration, and therefore needed constant supervision. I remember going to awful places like Banstead and Friern Barnet to see him before a more humane place could be found to look after this genius, the State institutions which were free but horrifying; the private houses (and this was the early 1960's) cost from £100 to £200 per week, which my mother could not afford. At Friern Barnet the main door to the closed section of the institution would be unlocked to admit us into the inner, darker part. The padded cells, where he was several times incarcerated 'for his own good', had a menacing, dark and frightening finality about them. When my mother visited him, alone or with my brother and I, it necessitated a trip from Central London with several changes of bus - and she visited him every day of the years he was in home, hospital, mental home or institution. Sometimes bruised or with black eyes after fights between inmates, my father just couldn't recognize any of us, would make strange sounds and, because of a multiplicity of drugs, would have saliva coming out from his mouth. He had to take drugs against depression, outbursts, frustration; different colours, types, strengths; all to no avail – he died at 57, a cadaver before his time. Dignified to the end, he would stagger up on seeing my mother. Mary Rose sat on a pin, Mary Rose: a little joke between them.

From the first medical prognosis – wrong at first, as most of them were – as to the exact nature of his pornographic and debilitating illnesses, the advice was, "Go away to be looked after by private institutions that can cope". "How can I pay?" asked my mother. "Find the money," was the answer. Help did come to her from various sources, but was intermittent and irregular, certainly not consistent enough to pay the regular fees required. At an age younger than the current writer, he was already on the slope towards senility. In a corridor at the Priory Nursing Home in Priory Lane, Roehampton, a doctor after examining him for the first time, detachedly told my mother, "Premature Senility," and walked off down the corridor. My father was in his late 40s.

Before he began the period of permanent incarceration, because of his accelerating infirmities, he had tried rest as a possible cure to his need to be very, very active in very different artistic enterprises concurrently. He wrote to my mother very often from a priory in Aylesford, one of the first places he went to. Run by nuns, this institution provided quiet and tranquillity, where a person could be alone to relax and meditate, think and rest. He wrote a postcard to me almost on arrival in January 1958 at the place and because he spoke very often about the art of perspective, did a drawing of a strange fish with lots of bubbles, diminishing in size, emanating from its mouth. The writing on the postcard above the fish reads; 'Here's some perspective for you.'

After a period at home, he went to another institution when he became, despite the constant and dedicated love of my mother's attention, too much for her to handle. He wrote to me on a scrap of paper:

Dear Sebby,

This isn't a letter. It isn't even a note. It's a notelet.

But it brings my love to you and wishes you all the best for the next few weeks - and after.

Love to you

From Daddy

I treasure these and the other few letters and cards I had from him, because I know now the mental and physical agonies he went through. At the time a teenager, and younger, I was sometimes unaware of his real illnesses and their toll on him and my mother. He was my father whom I loved so much that the very memory of him and his dignified forebearances can bring tears to me. My mother was once told by a relation that she should feel 'honoured' to be able to care for someone so special and that the hand of God was on her and him. This eyewash was, of course, at one remove from actually seeing the pencil falling from his hand on trying to draw or on hearing incomprehensible sounds through his drugged system. This 'honour' was a 24 hour hell, especially when my father could not sleep, for the clock of his physical body started to become very different from ours as soon as the drugs - he called them bombs - became the sine qua non of his existence. From the early, retreat-like weekends away to try to expunge, even temporarily, the need to work, to the middle period of constant nursing at home, to the final and deadly slope to full, unadulterated hell alive, the period of decline took some 8 years. For the month preceding the departure to a series of institutions, homes, psychiatric homes, the tension we lived under in our house in Wallington was awful. He would walk all over the house, up and down the stairs, get into bed and out again, get dressed and undressed, want a pencil to draw, paint and then not want to, call my mother the moment she had just put him to bed at 2.30 p.m. in the afternoon, asking to put back on the clothes she had just taken off and so on. When people came to see him - admirers, students, fellow writers, painters - he would be still for a while then with a movement of his eye, indicated to my mother he had had enough and leave. Always extremely polite and well mannered, he had a fairly short tolerance of other people. Simply put, the 'feel' of the other, unless it were someone who was patently dear, an old friend or family member, didn't really quite fit in. The loyal friends and family watching helplessly as the illnesses took their course towards his death in November 1968, were always profoundly and genuinely moved by the sight of his decline and many offered to help as he got worse.

When the arbitrary shouting and loud cries which would echo around the house, and the constant and debilitating demands upon my mother became no longer tenable, it was a strange sort of relief and sadness that came to settle over us all. There laid in his work room on his old mahogany table, (on which a thousand illustrations had been born, where *Titus Alone* was written, where *The Glassblowers* poems were put together for the collection, on which the great *Treasure Island, Ancient Mariner, Quest for Sita* were drawn) his attempts at drawings, some of them waiting for his vitality that was never to return. The smell of paint, charcoal, crayons, pencils, canvasses, paper, his utensils, his own world, at which he was a master, sat like Miss Haversham's wedding guests' room. The tragedy of it all', the waste of those last years, the languishing of his talent. When I visit his grave, which I do frequently, I am uplifted when reading his words: 'To live at all is miracle enough' and feel that he did live, he did have a happy marriage, he was someone who left a legacy that is for the nation to see, feel and experience. If the establishment, the museums, are so insensitive to his contribution to English Art, if they choose to wear blindfolds, and if his works do not provoke an excitement in them, moved and changed by his contribution, then they are as foolish as I hold them to be.

He died in a home in Burford near Oxford, run by a wonderfully committed uncle of mine who as a man wanted to care for the lonely and old and as a doctor to help them painlessly end their days. On days that I visited my father, towards the end, there he would be, sitting somewhere in a row of octogenarians in his fifties, looking the same age as them. In the final days I went to see him and on reaching out my hand for his, tears welled up in me, but I controlled myself and pretended to be interested in the other patients, hiding, I thought, my depth of sorrow. On regaining my composure, I looked at him and his moist eyes opened and on recognizing me, he cried and mouthed the word 'Sebby'. I never saw him alive again and I did not want to see him in death. Two days after my last visit we all went back to my uncle's home the moment we heard he'd died. Death **was** for him such sweet sorrow, for he had had enough: nearly eight years of shifting from place to place at a stage before L Dopa. He had had an operation on his skull - a practice for Parkinson's disease now abandoned, which did no good, left a dent in his forehead the size of a golfball and did not keep the intense sporadic shakings at bay, as had been promised, and which had left my mother in the deepest of dilemmas as to whether to put my father through the terrifying ordeal.

My uncle, who died recently, was the kindest and most considerate of Christians and the token £25 weekly my mother paid for the last year or so of my father's life, was a relief financially, but also in a spiritual sense, as he promoted the ideal of the Hospice, long before this idea became as well known. Assisted by his wife, Dr Gilmore gave 'The Close' an atmosphere of love and caring, free of bureaucratic pettinesses, concentrating on the things that really matter; the little appropriate joke at breakfast, the helping hand of real care. I have personally canonized him, for my Uncle James brought relief to my mother and love to my father when he really needed it.

At the funeral in Burpham in Sussex, where Dr. Peake had lived and practised, grown old and died, and where he, his wife, my father's brother and sister-in-law and now my mother and father lie together, there was a large congregation. Later, at the Memorial Service in St. James's, Piccadilly, Sir John Clements, an old friend, read some of my father's poetry from the lectern. He was buried at the age of 57 looking nearer 90, leaving behind him over 10,000 drawings, 200 oil paintings, books, poems, short stories, illustrations, plays, film scripts, stage designs, and ideas that are as radiant in concept and execution as they were from their inception. Projects now underway in film, play and written word began to a great extent in the little cluster of houses that make up Warningcamp and Burpham, nestling under the South Downs beside the Arun on the chalk soil of the hilly beauty of Sussex near the sea.

At times when I remember the man I loved that was my father, I produce from the past the naive but simple, profound but evocative, Catholic prayer that we said at Vauxblets, kneeling on the stone floors in our pyjamas with the windows of the dormitory wide open for the good of the soul. We would pray out loud in unison:

Jesus, Mary and Joseph, I give thee my heart and my soul

Jesus, Mary and Joseph, assist me in my last agony

Jesus, Mary and Joseph, may I breathe forth my soul in thy
  sweet company.

This helps sometimes, because it evokes naivete and the simplicity of childish belief, but it also lies deep in received belief that remains and keeps me cool when I want to explode with the unfairness of the story I have just told.

Boy on a donkey, 1948